The Best Bachelorette Party Book

Becky Long

Meadowbrook Press

Distributed by Simon & Schuster
New York

Library of Congress Cataloging-in-Publication Data
Long, Becky.
    The best bachelorette party book / by Becky Long.
        p.   cm.
    ISBN 0-88166-368-9 (Meadowbrook)—ISBN 0-671-31819-5 (Simon & Schuster)
    1. Bachelorette parties. I. Title.

GV1462.7.B33 L66 2000
793.2—dc21   00-025100

Managing Editor: Christine Zuchora-Walske
Copyeditor: Joseph Gredler
Proofreader: Megan McGinnis
Production Manager: Paul Woods
Desktop Publishing: Danielle White
Cover Art: Jack Lindstrom
Illustrations: Laurel Aiello

© 2000 by Becky Long

Published by Meadowbrook Press, 5451 Smetana Drive, Minnetonka, MN 55343

www.meadowbrookpress.com

BOOK TRADE DISTRIBUTION by Simon & Schuster, a division of Simon and
Schuster, Inc., 1230 Avenue of the Americas, New York, NY 10020

04   10 9 8 7

Printed in the United States of America

CONTENTS

Chapter 3: Far-from-Lame Games

Chapter 4: The Blushing Bride

Chapter 5: Eat, Drink, and Be Married

Chapter 6: Gifts and Favors

Chapter 7: More Party Ideas

Introduction

Anyone who's ever planned a wedding understands how stressful it can be. Getting things right and following the rules of etiquette can be overwhelming. The bachelorette party gives the bride-to-be a chance to decompress. It gives her an opportunity to temporarily throw the rules of etiquette to the wind and just have fun. It also gives her a chance to spend quality party time with her closest friends and relatives.

The Best Bachelorette Party Book features hundreds of clever party-planning ideas that are sure to please fun-hungry bachelorettes. It includes original party themes, unique invitations, hilarious games, yummy recipes, and much more to make your job as hostess a no-brainer. From conservative to crazy, you'll find games and activities perfectly suited to your partygoers' personalities.

You can send guests on video scavenger hunts or make the bride blush with condom-adorned apparel for her special evening. You can host a traveling bachelorette party out of town, gather in the comfort of someone's home, or spend the night hopping around to your favorite bars and nightclubs. Your toughest challenge will be deciding which ideas to leave out. Whatever your style, this book will help make your bachelorette party a night to remember.

PARTY PLANNING 101

The key to success is thorough planning and organization. To get the ball rolling, you'll first want to speak with the guest of honor about your intentions. Discuss the guest list and any activities the bride should know about. If you're planning a surprise party, remember that the bride's calendar is typically cluttered in the final days before the wedding. You should clear the date with her and still keep the party details a secret. Keep in mind that she's likely to be embarrassed by some of the activities—that's part of the fun. But try to avoid anything that might upset her.

Selecting a Date and Time

The bride should let you know when she'll be available. Bachelorette parties used to be held quite close to the wedding day, but trends have changed. It's much more common to see the party scheduled at least a week before the wedding, if not earlier.

Before confirming a date, make sure the party location has been secured. You should also check with guests to make sure the date works for them. Keep in mind, however, that the odds of finding a date that works for everyone are about as good as seeing those lovely aquamarine bridesmaids dresses worn again after the wedding day.

Determining Party Style

There are some important guidelines to consider when planning a bachelorette party. First, make sure the party's tone matches the bride's personality. Stage an event that leaves the bride blushing but not mortified. Remember, your goal is to have fun, blow off steam, and create fond memories—not nightmares—for the guest of honor.

Also, keep in mind the general disposition of your guests. Do they know one another? If not, you might begin the party with icebreaker games to help them get acquainted. Do they share any interests? Use this valuable information to design a party that everyone will enjoy.

The Guest List

You may be wondering what one means, exactly, by *bachelorette*. A popular dictionary defines the term as a young, unmarried woman. This seems both vague and unnecessarily restrictive. What if you wanted to invite the bride's mother, the groom's grandmother, or some older friends? The *bride* should get to choose who should be a bachelorette on her special night.

Remember to carefully consider your plans when assembling the guest list. Make sure the activities are compatible with the guests. Once the list is finalized, have the bride fill out the guest sheet (page 118) including the bachelorettes' names, mailing addresses, and phone numbers.

Invitations

Invitations should be sent at least three to four weeks in advance, if possible. You'll want to provide plenty of time for guests to arrange for travel, child care, and so on.

Invitations should include the guest of honor's name, party date, time, location, and directions. You should write R.S.V.P. on the invitations to ensure an accurate head count. You'll also want to make sure each guest received the invitation, so avoid writing, "Regrets only." Invite them to respond either way.

Remember to include your phone number and a date by which you would like guests to respond. You may also need to include special information about hotel reservations, dress, party themes, and so on. Finally, if you're sending an unusual invitation and want to see how it travels through the mail, try sending it to yourself first.

Location, Location, Location

Sometimes the most important ingredient in a successful party-planning recipe is the venue. In its broadest sense, *location* refers to the city in which the party will be staged. *Venue* refers to the actual gathering place within that city.

The guest list will influence your location decision. If most bachelorettes are clustered in a certain area that's also convenient for the bride, then arrangements will be fairly simple. On the other hand, if guests are scattered across several states, a central location—perhaps another city—might be the best solution. Choose a venue that's large enough to accommodate all the guests, yet not so large that you lose group intimacy.

In some cases your venue can provide the entertainment. For example, you might buy tickets to see a male revue or comedy act. Many restaurants offer entertainment, particularly Japanese steak houses and fondue restaurants. While the local watering hole remains the perennial favorite among bachelorettes, you may want to check out the following options:

- Spas
- Wineries
- Malls
- Ball parks
- Hotels
- Parks
- Breweries
- Skating rinks
- Boats
- Theaters
- Beaches
- Zoos

Who Should Guide Your Sleigh Tonight?

Transportation arrangements are crucial, especially if you'll be drinking. The bottom line is that drinking and driving do not mix. Take the time to coordinate safe and reliable transportation. You'll then be free to enjoy the festivities without the risk of tragedy.

If you don't plan to include alcohol as part of your evening's activities, then transportation becomes less a safety issue and more a matter of convenience and camaraderie. Either way, here are some options to consider:

- Designated drivers
- Limousine service
- Taxis
- Chartered bus
- Rented van or school bus (with hired driver)
- Subway, trolley, buses, or other public transportation

Another way to avoid putting guests behind the wheel after they've been drinking is to make the fun come to you. Host the party in the comfort of your home and have a sober driver take everyone home, or invite guests to spend the night. If a hotel near your venue provides a shuttle service, you might rent a room for the party, have guests walk to the various activities, and use the shuttle service when you're ready to call it a night.

Footing the Bill

You need to consider how the fun will be financed. Whichever option you choose, communicate clearly to your guests the costs involved and eliminate any extravagant activities that might preclude participation. Here are a few options:

The Really Rich Way

If you're dripping with money, you could foot the entire bill for the evening's festivities. Chances are you already have your own limousine and chauffeur.

The Meet-You-Halfway Way

This method lets you pick up a designated portion of the party expenses. These might include invitations, facility rental, entertainment, favors, and refreshments. Or, you could host a warm-up party in your home and serve drinks on the house. Guests would then pay for their drinks and snacks during the evening of barhopping. You could also consider recruiting an assistant hostess and splitting the expenses. If you're having the party at a restaurant, you could ask guests to purchase their main courses while you provide complimentary dessert and champagne.

The Split-the-Works Way

If money's tight, you could consider having everyone go Dutch treat. As hostess, your role would be reduced to event coordinator without carrying the additional burden of financing the festivities.

The Perfect Party Checklist

After you've taken the time to visualize your party from beginning to end, use the following checklist to help organize and track your preparations. You may want to photocopy it and carry it with you, checking things off as you go. Note that some items may not apply to your particular party plan. Feel free to add any details unique to your bachelorette party.

Three months before the party:
- Call the bride to discuss a date and time.
- Brainstorm about style and theme.
- Formulate a preliminary guest list with mailing addresses and phone numbers.
- Determine a location and secure a venue.
- Hire entertainment professionals (musicians, dancers, caterers, and so on).
- Plan activities.
- Secure transportation and/or lodging.

Two months before the party:
- Confirm the guest list.
- Select or design invitations.
- Assemble your favorite recipes.
- Send guests a card informing them to keep the date open.

One month before the party:
- Prepare and mail invitations.
- Select decorations.
- Begin searching for the perfect gift for your guest of honor.

One week before the party:
- Review invitation responses and finalize the guest list.
- Secure necessary prizes and props for scheduled activities.
- Purchase table service (plates, cups, napkins, flatware, and so on).

- Prepare party favors.
- Buy film.
- Finalize the menu and create a shopping list for ingredients.
- Stock the bar for an at-home party.

Two days before the party:
- Wrap the bride's gift.
- Purchase necessary food items.
- Secure plenty of ice and coolers if you're transporting beverages.
- Locate necessary serving dishes and utensils.

One day before the party:
- Decorate the party venue with everything except balloons.
- Prepare any menu items that can be made ahead of time.
- Have cash on hand for tips and other needs.

The day of the party:
- Prepare last-minute menu items and remove pre-made items from the freezer.
- Inflate balloons and complete decorations.
- Dress at least one hour before the party is scheduled to begin.
- Light the candles and turn on some music to welcome the guests.
- Have fun!

FUN PARTY THEMES

Theme planning will give your party a distinct personality. Think about fun ways to coordinate the festivities using the bride's occupation, hobbies, honeymoon destination, and so on as starting points. Your theme can be woven into every party detail or lightly sprinkled throughout various activities. Below you'll find suggestions for theme parties complete with invitations, activities, favors, and general party tips.

Rubber Bash

It's time to pull out your rubber raincoats and rubber boots. You can leave the umbrellas at home—after all, this is a bachelorette *party*, not a bridal *shower*.

Invitations
Using a permanent felt-tip marker, write party details on inflated condoms. Then deflate the condoms and attach note cards that read "Blow

me." A second option would involve gluing several rolled-up condoms to the front of each invitation. Attach a piece of ribbon to the bottom of each condom to make the condoms resemble a bouquet of balloons. A third option is to send custom-designed Rubbergrams to each guest. Order them online at www.rubbergrams.com. Your personalized Rubbergram invitations will arrive in plastic jars that guests will be instructed to open and fill with water. They'll be amazed as a condom emerges and inflates to reveal party details!

Party Scene

This is a party where anything rubber goes. Hang prophylactic balloons from the ceiling with rubber bands. (Try the glow-in-the-dark kind.) Use a rubber plant as a centerpiece. Insert condom *cock*tail stirrers in drinks (page 93). Serve party foods in Rubbermaid containers and invite guests to package their gifts in the same. Award a rubber ducky or jar of rubber cement to the bachelorette who presents the most creative packaging. The bride enjoys the added bonus of using these packages for practical purposes after the party. For an activity that stays in theme, try rubber-stamping gift items for the bride. Also see the Condom Contest (page 40) or play Blow Job (page 46).

Favors

Send each guest home with a pair of rubber gloves. Or, create designer rubber jewelry for each guest (page 102).

Get *Lei-d*

It's time for a bachelorette luau—an especially appropriate theme if the bride is lucky enough to be traveling to Hawaii for her honeymoon.

Invitations

Attach invitations to plastic leis. Suggest that bachelorettes wear the leis to the party along with Hawaiian shirts and other beach attire.

Party Scene

Travel to a beach or decorate the party scene to resemble a beach. Put the bride in a grass skirt and matching grass veil. Buy extra grass skirts to decorate the bar and trash cans. Don't forget the tiki torches. Serve shrimp presented on a palm tree made from pineapples. Core the pineapples and stack them on a pole to form a tree trunk. Carefully anchor the pole to a wooden base. To make palm branches, attach real branches to the top of the trunk using floral picks. Use decorative picks to attach the shrimp to the tree trunk. For dessert, serve fruit kebabs along with a delicious fruit dip (page 67). Also, check out the Piña Colada Cake (page 76), Blue Hawaiian drink recipe (page 82), Sex-on-the-Beach shot recipe (page 91), and Get *Lei-d* drink recipe (page 85).

Favors

Give each guest a custom-printed T-shirt that reads "I Got *Lei-d* at (bride's name)'s Bachelorette Party." You could also design your own using fabric paints. Or, fill fishnet stockings with trinkets and candy.

Bevy of Bridesmaids

Here's the perfect opportunity for bachelorettes to actually wear a bridesmaid's dress again! Instruct each guest to choose the most embarrassing one she owns for this unique costume party.

Invitations

For the front of your invitations, make copies of an old wedding picture that includes bridesmaids. Fill speech bubbles near the bridesmaids' mouths with funny comments such as "As if this dress isn't bad enough, I have good shoes dyed to match it!" or "Can you believe my best friend made me wear *this*?"

Party Scene

This party should definitely be held in a public place. Award costume prizes such as "The Best Preserved," "The Best Color," and "The Most Flattering." Make a special toast each time a stranger comments on the dresses.

Favors

Give each guest a small bridesmaid's bouquet to carry with her throughout the evening. As the party winds down, present each bridesmaid with a never-been-worn dyed pump filled with candy and other trinkets. Wrap the shoes in cellophane and tie each with a pretty bow.

Last Rites

At this party bachelorettes mourn the passing of the bride's single days by staging funeral-like yet fun-loving activities.

Invitations
Etch the party details on card stock cut into the shape of a tombstone.

Party Scene
Ask guests to wear black and the bride to wear white. Hire a hearse to transport the bride to the party location while guests follow in a car procession with headlights on. If you hire a band for the party, ask it to play a funeral march in the bride's honor. Have guests eulogize the bride with embarrassing stories from her past.

Favors
Make a condom corsage for each guest and a coordinating veil and train for the bride (page 50). Also check out the rosebud favors (page 104).

This Is Your Life

Enjoy a blast through the bride's past in a hysterical walk down memory lane. Try to keep the details a secret for this one.

Invitations

Select a funny photo of the bride as a cover. Enclose a self-addressed stamped envelope and ask guests to mail copies of other funny photos. Slip a few beans into each invitation to remind guests not to *spill the beans* about the party's intentions.

Party Scene

Enlarge the funny photos, hang them as posters, and challenge bachelorettes to a Caption Contest (page 31). Arrange for special guests to make surprise appearances in the "This Is Your Life" portion of the party. Recruit a favorite teacher, coach, prom date, or long-distance friend of the bride. For real laughs, have someone pretend to be the bride's favorite teen idol. Seat the bride in the center of the room and have an MC tell stories while surprise guests remain hidden in an adjoining room. Keep the bride in suspense as long as possible, then ask her to identify the surprise guest.

If you're heading out to celebrate, arrange to have an unflattering photo of the groom projected in larger-than-life proportions on a wall. Make sure everyone knows the geeky-looking guy is the groom. Assemble a memory basket for the bride (page 98) or create a funny video that features pictures of the bride's childhood. Secure photos from her parents and other relatives. You could play the video the night of the party and present it to the bride as a gift.

Favors

Give each bachelorette an armband garter to wear the night of the party. Attach a button that features a funny picture of the bride and the party date.

Honeymoon Prelude

You don't have to be invited on the honeymoon to enjoy the sights and sounds of the bride's dreamy destination. Recreate it as the perfect backdrop to your bachelorette gathering. For example, if the bride is headed to Italy, you could host a "That's Amore" party.

Invitations

Write party details on post cards depicting the honeymoon spot, or send party details on a tag attached to an item symbolizing the destination. For example, invitations to the "That's Amore" party could be embellished with pasta and tips on how to say funny phrases such as "Buzz off, garlic breath" in Italian.

Party Scene

Browse through travel guides for party ideas. Ask guests to bring theme-related gifts that can be taken on the honeymoon. For the "That's Amore" party, an Italian restaurant would be the obvious choice. The chef might even be able to bake bread in a festive bachelorette party shape. Canvas your tables in red, white, and green—the colors of Italy's flag. For place cards, write guests' names on lasagna noodles. Keep the vino flowing while Italian music or "How to Speak Italian" tapes play in the background. You might want to ask each bachelorette to bring a favorite pasta recipe to share with the bride. Fill a colander with goodies such as an Italian cookbook and novelty-shaped pasta (page 60). To really spice things up, throw in red, white, and green panties. Also check out the Italian Stallion shot recipe (page 88). As a gift for the bride, you could also play Pack Her Bags (page 98) or make a honeymoon scrapbook (page 101).

Favors
Provide keepsakes reminiscent of the romantic getaway. For the "That's Amore" party, give each bachelorette a heart-shaped candle or a fancy bottle filled with body oils and splashes (page 101).

Striptease

Strippers are the classic ingredients of the traditional bachelorette party.

Invitations
Buy some paper dolls or make your own out of card stock paper. Use a body outline from a child's coloring book as a template. Write party details on the doll's body and use cut-out clothing for a cover. Guests will need to strip the doll to find out party secrets.

Party Scene

Hire a stripper to make a special appearance at your party or make reservations to see exotic dancers. You could lead bachelorettes to this destination by having them follow a trail of clothing. Serve chicken *strips* (page 56).

Favors

Provide guests with crisp dollar bills for tipping the dancers, or visit an adult novelty store to find items that strip.

Pamper Party

Treat your bachelorette revelers to a night of luxury and decadence.

Invitations

Place slips of paper containing party details in champagne glasses wrapped in tulle. Arrange to have them delivered on a silver tray by a gentleman dressed in a tuxedo. If that's not feasible, mail scented invitations attached to powder puffs.

Party Scene

In preparation for a night on the town, arrange for a masseuse and manicurist to be on hand for the warm-up party. Or, have guests paint each other's nails using a wide variety of nail polishes that you've provided. Encourage guests to wear their most luxurious robes and slippers for the pamper party and to bring a change of clothes for later festivities. Serve umbrella drinks and bonbons.

Favors
Provide inexpensive sunglasses as party favors so your bachelorettes will be able to endure the paparazzi.

Find the *Heart-On*

Bachelorettes will enjoy an evening filled with *heart-on* fun.

Invitations
Include a headline that reads "Can you find the *heart on* this invitation?" Be sure to dot each *i* with a small heart.

Party Scene
Arrange a search for *heart-ons* by placing heart-shaped cutouts on a variety of objects. The guest who finds the most cutouts wins. To decorate, hang hearts in various shapes and sizes from ceilings and doorways. Embrace a popular tradition by baking a charm cake for a centerpiece. Originally, charms such as hearts, bells, and rings were attached to ribbons and baked into the cake. Each charm symbolized something different. Bridesmaids would retrieve the charms to determine their fortunes. For example, the bridesmaid who found the ring was believed to be the next to wed. You could tie ribbons to various trinkets with

humorous implications. For example, the bachelorette who pulls the ribbon attached to a condom with a hole in it may be the next to have a baby. You could prepare a simple bundt cake or try the Kahlua Cake (page 75). Make fancy ice cubes with heart designs (page 93).

Favors
Give guests anything with a *heart on* it.

Winetasting

A winetasting bachelorette party can make for a really *grape* evening.

Invitations
Design invitations to read like wine labels asking guests to join you at your favorite bar, restaurant, or chateau.

Party Scene
You don't have to be a wine expert to pull off a great party. Consult a book about wine for party ideas. You could provide a variety of wines or ask each guest to bring a bottle. Distribute glasses and let the tasting begin. Ask each guest to report her first impressions about each wine's color, smell, and taste. Award prizes for the most creative responses. Provide bread and water for cleansing guests' palates between bottles. To decorate, use empty wine bottles as candle holders and accent with inexpensive grapevine wreaths and grape clusters. Check out the delicious recipe for Wine and Cheese Fondue (page 66).

After the tasting, host a wineglass-decorating contest. Use paints made specifically for glass so the designs will last long after the wine has disappeared. Also, you and your guests might want to collectively purchase a wine rack for the bride and have each guest bring her favorite vintage with a label attached indicating the circumstances under which the bottle should be opened. For example, a guest could request that her bottle be uncorked on the couple's fifth wedding anniversary or after they move into a new house.

Favors
Send each guest home with a corkscrew. Attach a note card that reads, "Thanks for screwing around with us at (bride's name)'s bachelorette party." You could also hire an artist to paint guests' caricatures on wineglasses.

Variation
Make it a wine and music party. Invite each guest to bring a CD for the couple in addition to a favorite bottle of wine.

Some Like It Hot

Here's a theme that will spice things up.

Invitations
Attach party details to a package of spicy seasoning or a box of Hot Tamales candies.

Party Scene

Decorate with lots of dried red chili peppers. Invite guests to bring the bride anything they feel will spice up her marriage. Creative options might include sexy lingerie or a Mexican cookbook. You might plan to give the bride a spice rack and ask each guest to bring a bottle of her favorite spice to fill the rack. Serve hot, spicy foods or go out to a restaurant that serves the same.

Favors

Personalize an oven mitt for each bachelorette or send each guest home with a jar of homemade salsa.

A-Traveling We Will Go

A bachelorette party that goes on the road can provide a lifetime of memories.

Invitations

Insert party details into luggage tags. Include a detailed itinerary of your trip so guests will be clear on times, dress, costs, and so on. A thoughtful hostess will keep the expenses within reason, making sure that no guest feels overtaxed or unable to attend.

Party Scene

This party could be designed for an intimate few or for several guests. It could take you far from home or just around the corner. For example, you could make plans to attend a male revue in Las Vegas or opt for a night of barhopping and hotel accommodations within stumbling distance. For added fun, keep the destination a surprise to both guests and bride, though this might be tricky. There will be many details to lock down before you leave, and once you set foot on foreign soil, even the most trivial preparations will be greatly appreciated. Welcome each guest to the party with a disposable camera so that she can record her version of the bachelorette activities. Challenge guests to see who can collect the most out-of-town business cards from eligible bachelors. Keep in mind that off-season travel packages and group discounts may be available. Also, make sure that everyone has a passport if necessary.

Favors
Make inexpensive tote bags for each guest from men's boxer shorts (page 106). You could also distribute the totes ahead of time, specifying that guests bring no more than what they can fit into the tote, if feasible.

French Flair

What could be more fun than a bachelorette soiree that pays tribute to the country known for its kiss?

Invitations
Attach party details to anything that has to do with Pepe Le Pew or the Eiffel Tower. You could also write the party information on loaves of French bread to be hand delivered.

Party Scene

Serve French onion soup and decadent pastries at home or make reservations at a French restaurant. Bon appétit! Toast the bride with a bottle of Dom Perignon to really impress your guests. Also, check out the French Kiss shot recipe (page 87). You could dress the guest of honor in a French maid's costume and make berets out of felt for the guests to wear the night of the party. Provide French manicures and invite guests to bring personal presents for the bride's boudoir.

Favors

Say *bon soir* with tiny bottles of French perfume or personalized French maid aprons.

Variation

Head to the French Quarter in New Orleans and give your party a Mardi Gras twist.

Take the Plunge

Celebrate the wedding plunge with a pool party!

Invitations

Glue invitations to the bottoms of inexpensive flip-flops.

Party Scene

Arrange for a clambake accompanied by Beach Boys music and plenty of rum punch (page 81). To decorate, ask each guest to incorporate a child's inflatable pool toy into her present for the bride. Serve chips and dips in plastic beach toys such as sand pails and sailboats. Give each bachelorette a pair of "beer goggles" to wear the night of the party.

Favors

Send each guest home with an inexpensive pool raft or swim cap. Or, decorate inexpensive flip-flops with fabric flowers. Simply clip the stems from the flowers and attach them to the shoe's toe piece with hot glue.

Variation

Give your pool party a sunny twist by throwing a "Girls Just Wanna Have Sun" party at a beach or pool. Incorporate *sun*sational ideas such as sunscreen and sunglasses into invitations, prizes, and party favors.

Chick-Flickathon

Try a girls' night *in*. This relaxing break from tradition might be just what your bachelorette crew is looking for.

Invitations

Design invitations to resemble movie tickets, or play off the pajama party theme by placing a picture of the bride as a little girl wearing pajamas on the cover.

Party Scene

Invite guests to bring their favorite comfort foods and recipes. Supply the froo-froo drinks (page 82), large bowls of popcorn, and a hefty supply of chick flicks to generate a night of good old-fashioned pajama party fun. Canvas the venue with movie posters. Play the following Hollywood drinking game. Sit in a circle and take turns naming actresses. After a name is called, go around the circle one at a time and have guests name movies starring the actress. Limit the response time to fifteen seconds. Anyone who draws a blank before her time expires has to drink. You could also require guests to take a swig for each correct movie that other guests are able to name. Another fun activity is the Who Game (page 46).

Favors

Send guests home with popcorn tins, fuzzy slippers, or personalized nightshirts.

Variation

Add the drama of the Academy Awards to your special evening. Send fancy invitations asking each guest to come dressed as her favorite actress from a chick flick. Present silly awards such as "Most Dramatic" to the guest who cries the most during the movie. Her trophy could be a box of tissues. Boys beware: Guests might want to make this party an annual tradition.

Search Party

Bachelorettes will enjoy an evening of intrigue as they attempt to solve a mystery. This party is somewhat labor-intensive but well worth the effort.

Invitations

Write party details in small type on a note card and include a magnifying glass to help guests read the type. Or, print party details on the back of a bookmark enclosed in an old mystery novel. You can find inexpensive books at flea markets, garage sales, and used bookstores.

Party Scene

Divide guests into two teams and send them on an evening of barhopping and mystery solving. At each stop, the hostess reads a riddle to help guests find the clue that she has planted at each location. Clues should be easily identifiable. For example, each clue could have a paper cutout shaped like a wedding cake attached to it. Teams search the location for the clue, and five points are awarded to the team that finds it. Teams then proceed to the next stop. Bachelorettes have to figure out the significance of each clue in order to solve the final mystery. The team that solves the final mystery gets an additional ten points. The team with the most points at the end wins! Here's an example:

Riddle #1: "While this old flame once turned the bride's heart to mush, she now says goodbye with a single flush."

Answer: This riddle should lead guests to the women's bathroom to find Clue #1. "Something old" will be found next to one of the toilets: a picture of the bride's former boyfriend attached to the wedding cake cutout.

Riddle #2: "You can lead a horse to water, but only this guy can make him drink."

Answer: This riddle should lead guests to a bartender who has the wedding cake cutout in his pocket. The bartender will make them Clue #2—"something new"—a new drink or shot.

Riddle #3: "A man with a microphone holds our next clue; go see him to find what he has for you."

Answer: This should lead guests to the DJ who's been given the wedding cake cutout. The DJ will then announce over the sound system that he holds Clue #3—"something borrowed"—an adult video or some other embarrassing item that's been reserved for the bride.

Riddle #4: "You haven't seen this guy since stop number two; find the right one and he'll know what to do."

Answer: Guests should find the bartender wearing the wedding cake cutout. He will make them Clue #4—"something blue"—a drink made with blue curacao.

Riddle #5: "If you don't behave, he'll throw you out, but first solve your mystery beyond a reasonable doubt."

Answer: If guests are on their toes, they'll ask the bouncer for the final clue. He'll be wearing the wedding cake cutout with a lucky sixpence attached to it for the bride to put in her shoe on her wedding day. The mystery is solved! It's time to celebrate!

Decorate the traveling van to resemble the Mystery Machine from *Scooby Doo*. Ask your bachelorette detectives to wear trench coats.

Favors

Buy a small photo album for each guest. Include funny labels, such as "Gathering Evidence," "Exhibit A," and "Guilty" to help them identify their keepsake photos.

FAR-FROM-LAME GAMES

Games and activities are usually the highlights of a bachelorette party. They help break the ice and establish a foundation of camaraderie and trust. The most important factor to consider when selecting activities is the group's general disposition. If you feel guests would be more than mildly embarrassed by a certain game, choose something else. Your goal is to make sure everyone has a good time. The following games and activities range from fairly conservative to somewhat outrageous. Secure the necessary props and prizes well ahead of time, and acquaint yourself thoroughly with each game and activity to avoid problems the night of the party.

Icebreakers

These games are designed to be played near the beginning of the party. They'll help guests get better acquainted.

What Am I?

Attach a slip of paper featuring a word having to do with love, sex, or marriage to each guest's back. Don't let guests see their own words. The object of the game is for each guest to discover her word by asking yes or no questions to other guests. Guests are only allowed to respond with a simple yes or no. Remove or cover all mirrors to make sure there's no cheating. Award a prize to the guest who correctly guesses her word first.

Variation: Help guests learn more about the bride and groom by attaching slips of paper containing the couple's personal information to each guest's back. You might include where the couple met, their honeymoon destination, their favorite movies, and so on.

Pin the Privates on the Pinup

Cut game pieces for each bachelorette from construction paper using the anatomically correct template (page 119). Decorate the pieces ahead of time (or challenge guests to do so at the party) and place them in a new pair of men's underwear. As guests arrive, have each one select a game piece from the undies and write her name on it. Instruct guests to wear their pieces until the game begins. When it's time, have guests gather round the male pinup for a racy version of Pin the Tail on the Donkey. The same rules apply. Blindfold each guest and have her attempt to pin her piece to the appropriate spot on the pinup. Award prizes for "Closest to the Pin" and "Not Even Close." If heading out for a night on the town, have guests wear their game pieces.

Variation #1: Pin cocktail weenies on the pinup.

Variation #2: Look for "Pin the Macho on the Man" at your local adult novelty store.

Caption Contest

This game will provide fun and instant decorations. Contact the bride's family and friends to help gather a collection of the funniest, most embarrassing photographs of the bride. Display them in several locations at the party. Assign each guest a photograph and ask her to write a funny caption for it. Award prizes for the funniest contributions. Gather the photographs and captions in a special keepsake album and present it to the bride after the party.

Variation: Have guests write captions for pictures selected from *Playgirl*.

Lost Lovers' Lane

Have guests unscramble names of the bride's old boyfriends and junior-high crushes. For example, "lbdeary tishm" would be Bradley Smith. Award a prize to the guest who deciphers the most names correctly.

Brain Cell Challenge

Help the bride pack for her honeymoon by asking each guest to suggest an item—silly or otherwise—that the bride should include in her suitcase. Have each guest repeat the list of previously mentioned items before adding hers. If a guest forgets an item, she must drop out. Award a prize to the bachelorette who is able to recite the longest list of items correctly.

Variation: Instead of suitcase items, have guests create lists of unique sexual positions, forms of birth control, or creative marital advice.

Bust the Piñata

Order a piñata from Provocative Piñatas at 800-PINATAS (800-746-2827) or online at www.provocativepinatas.com. You can also make your own piñata in the shape of male anatomy by following these directions.

Supplies:
- 5 12-inch round balloons
- masking tape
- newspaper
- flour
- water
- string
- skin-colored paint
- paintbrush

Directions: Inflate balloons and tape together as illustrated.

Tear newspaper into strips. Mix 4 cups flour to 4 cups water. Stir to form paste. Dip strips of newspaper in paste. Run strips between fingers to remove excess paste. Wrap strips on balloons to cover completely. Allow several days to dry. Once dry, pop balloons with pin. Cut small hole in top of piñata and insert string for hanging. Tie knot on inside to secure. Cut 3-inch-square flap on back side of each piñata and insert candy, condoms, and other bachelorette surprises. Seal flap with more newspaper strips dipped in paste. Allow to dry and paint piñata in skin-colored tones.

Fun-for-All Activities

These games and activities are designed to help you please everyone on your guest list. A basic format is provided for each event, but feel free to make changes that will better suit your bachelorettes. Most games can go from mild to wild quite easily.

Wedding Night Obstacle Course

Divide guests into two teams. Use a stopwatch to time each team member as she makes her way through the obstacle course. The team with the lowest total time wins. Make a sign identifying the various tasks each contestant must perform in her race against the clock. Examples might include the following:

- Putting on a wedding veil
- Proposing a toast and drinking a glass of champagne

- Eating a slice of wedding cake
- Throwing a bouquet over her shoulder to another team member (The bouquet must be caught before the guest moves on to the next obstacle.)
- Shaking hands with three members of the opposite team and thanking them for coming to *your* wedding
- Carrying a Ken doll over the threshold
- Hanging a "Do Not Disturb" sign on the door
- Chewing a candy cigarette *afterward*

Truth or Consequences

Set the stage for a night of hilarious antics by asking the bride to answer honestly a series of personal questions. Have her write down answers well in advance. The night of the party, ask the bachelorettes to guess how the bride responded to each question. If their answers don't match the bride's, they will be asked to pay the consequences. The success of this activity will largely depend on how well you match the questions and consequences to your guests' personalities. The more difficult the questions, the more likely your guests will have to pay the consequences. Here are some examples:

Sample Questions for the Bride:

- Who received your first romantic kiss?
- Who did you go out with on your first car date?
- Where did you go on your first date with your fiancé?
- How many children do you hope to have?

- If you had to be stranded on a deserted island with someone other than your fiancé, who would you choose?
- What do you feel is the perfect man's most important attribute?
- What puts you in the mood?
- What's your favorite love song?
- Where's the most unusual place you've done it?
- If one were to search for your virginity, where might she find it?

Sample Consequences for Contestants:
(Make sure you secure props well ahead of time.)

- List five household uses for a condom.
- Take a big swig of your drink and, before swallowing, provide a one-minute description of your most memorable romantic encounter.
- Give a three-minute description of how your real or imaginary husband proposed to you. Refer to him only as "Mr. Well-Hung Dude."
- Pretend you're the bride and skip to the future. Five-year-old Junior has just asked, "Where do babies come from?" Provide an original and descriptive answer.
- While blindfolded, draw a picture of your perfect man on a chalkboard or paper. (Occasionally pull the artist away from the chalkboard so she temporarily loses her bearings.)
- Carve an anatomically correct male body part from a banana with your teeth.
- Describe five major differences between you and a jock strap.

- Eat five crackers and then whistle a few bars of the bride's favorite love song.
- Make up a four-line rhyming poem about the bride and groom's honeymoon night.
- Write a lost-and-found ad for the newspaper about the loss of your virginity. Include where it was last seen and with whom.

Truth or Dare

It's time to see how well the bride knows her groom. Before the party, ask the groom a variety of personal questions. Examples might include, "What's your favorite family vacation memory?" or, "If you could change one thing about yourself, what would it be?" Write each question and its corresponding answer on an index card. On the back of each card, write a dare. At the party, give each guest an index card and have her ask the bride her question. If the bride answers incorrectly, she must perform the dare described on the back of the card. If she guesses correctly, the guest asking the question must perform the dare. Dares might include kissing an unknown guy's tattoo, combing a hairy man's chest, polishing a bald guy's head, and so on.

Variation: Give out small prizes rather than dares. For example, if the bride's answer matches her groom's, then she gets the prize. If it does not, the guest walks away with the spoils. You could also give the bride a green M&M (which she must immediately eat) for every right answer, and a piece of bubble gum (which she must chew throughout the game) for every wrong answer. She might be able to blow quite a large bubble by the end of the game!

Video Scavenger Hunt

Divide guests into teams and arrange for each team to have a video camera. Send them off to shoot footage of scenes related to love, sex, or marriage. Assign points for each piece of footage according to the level of difficulty. Give teams a list of options with designated point values. The team with the most points wins. Choose from the following assignments or make up your own:

- Team member purchasing something other than aspirin from a bathroom vending machine (*5 points*)
- Team member being serenaded by a stranger singing at least one full verse of a love song (*5 points*)
- Team members posing in a stranger's luxury sports car (*5 points*)
- Team member kissing a stranger in uniform (*10 points*)
- Team member securing a marriage proposal from a stranger on bended knee (*10 points*)
- Team members decorating a stranger's car with "Just Married" signs, tin cans, and so on (*10-20 points*, more points for more decorations)
- Team member clearing a busy dance floor for a first dance with a strange male after the dance has been announced on the club's main sound system (*15 points*)
- Team member removing the shirt of an unsuspecting man (*15 points* plus five bonus points if the person allows anything else to be removed)

- Team members toasting the bride next to a guy with the same first name as the groom (*15 points,* and the guy must show his driver's license on camera as proof of identification)

- Team member doing a body shot such as "Lick It, Slam It, Suck It" on page 89 (*20 points*)

- Team members cutting the labels from five different guys' underwear (*20 points*)

- Team members carrying a bellhop over the threshold of a honeymoon suite in an upscale hotel (*20 points* plus five bonus points if at least one team member doesn't emerge until the next morning)

Variation: Send the teams out with Polaroid cameras instead of video cameras. The pictures will be great additions to the bride's scrapbook.

Scavenger Hunt

This game is a lot like its video counterpart. However, the mission here is to return with tangible items. Divide guests into teams and send them out for a game of fetch. The team that gathers items worth the most points wins. Here are some ideas to get you started, but you'll have lots of fun coming up with your own:

5 points
- Rice (uncooked)
- Garter
- Bouquet
- Cake mix
- Champagne (*15 bonus points if there's enough for everyone*)

10 points

- Bride-and-groom plastic cake topper
- Toaster
- Bow tie
- Invitation from another wedding
- Men's boxer shorts (*20 bonus points if the man is still in them and that's all he's wearing*)

15 points

- Veil (not the bride's)
- Wedding photo
- "Do not disturb" sign
- Pack of personalized matches or a napkin from another wedding
- Adult video (*10 bonus points if a team member knows the ending*)

Tip: Have each team carry its booty in a tote bag made from men's boxer shorts (page 106).

Variation: Send guests on a scavenger hunt to find traditional anniversary gifts (page 117). For example, guests could return with a newspaper to satisfy the traditional first anniversary gift of paper. Set a time limit. The team that accumulates the most anniversary gifts wins.

Bimbo

This game resembles the traditional game of Bingo and adds fun to the present-opening process. Begin by giving each guest a blank Bimbo card. Make copies of the game card found on page 120. You may want to add photos of the bride in the free spaces on each card. Instruct guests to fill in the squares on their cards with names of presents they think the bride might receive at the bachelorette party. Examples could include lingerie, perfume, bath gel, and so on. If the bride opens any of these items, guests should mark their cards in the appropriate squares with green M&Ms. The first guest to mark five squares in a row either vertically, horizontally, or diagonally should yell, "Bimbo" to receive a prize!

Variation: Use this game as an icebreaker by having guests sign their names in the squares on each other's cards. Then have each guest write her name on a slip of paper and drop it in a basket. The hostess then selects the names one at a time and guests mark the corresponding squares on their cards with green M&M's. Award a prize to the first "Bimbo!"

Condom Contest

If you start with a bunch of bananas and add a box of nonlubricated condoms, what do you have? A zany activity that will leave your bachelorettes in stitches. The winning bachelorette will be the first to peel her banana, remove the condom from its package, and roll it correctly on the banana. Have plenty of paper towels or washcloths on hand for cleanup.

Paper Bag Theater

Divide guests into teams. Provide each team with a grocery bag filled with various props. Be sure each bag has the same number of props. Set a time limit and challenge teams to create skits about the bride and groom, using all the props. Award prizes to the best off—really off—Broadway production.

Art Appreciation

Give each guest a hardcover book, a blank piece of paper, and a crayon. Have each write her name on her piece of paper. Then instruct each guest to flip over her paper, set it on top of the book, and place both on top of her head. Next, have each guest draw a picture of the groom in his boxer shorts, using the paper on top of her head. When time expires, put the pictures in a pile and have the bride choose the one that most closely resembles her groom. Award a prize to the best Picasso in the group.

Love Drawings

Write down several names and phrases having to do with love, sex, or marriage on slips of paper and put them in a basket. One at a time, have each guest select a slip of paper and illustrate the name or phrase on a chalkboard or large piece of paper. The other guests try to guess what the drawing represents. The person who correctly identifies the name or phrase scores a point, and the person with the most points at the end wins a prize. You'll need to select a scorekeeper and set a time limit to keep things moving. Some suggested phrases include "birds and bees," "Mr. Right," and "Not tonight, I have a headache." You could also divide into teams, giving each a separate phrase basket and drawing supplies. The first team to guess their phrase correctly gets a point, and the team who gets the most points wins.

White Elephant Gift Exchange

Ask each guest to bring a wrapped white elephant gift having to do with love, sex, or marriage. Have guests sit in a circle and place the gifts in the center. Distribute several pie tins with a pair of dice in each. Ask each guest to roll the dice and then pass the tin to her right. If a guest rolls doubles, she may select a gift from the pile. Once the gifts have all been selected, give guests an opportunity to exchange their gifts with other guests by rolling doubles. You might want to set a time limit depending on the number of guests. When time is up, have guests open their gifts and describe how they'll put them to good use.

We're Looking for a Few Good Men

Host a gingerbread man decorating contest. Have gingerbread man cookies and a wide variety of decorating supplies on hand. After the cookies are decorated, have each guest introduce her man to the group and tell what makes him special. Give prizes to the most creative and humorous presentations. You might use categories such as "Best Dressed," "Most Impressive Body Part," and "Biggest Geek."

Crazy Tales

Tell guests that you've written a fill-in-the-blank story about how the bride and groom met or about their honeymoon. What you've actually done is designed an interesting plot line that requires guests to fill in important details. Ask guests one at a time to provide a needed word or phrase, but don't reveal the plot line. To make things more interesting, throw in special requests for items such as body parts, sizes, and names of old boyfriends. When guests have finished providing the necessary information to complete the story, have each guest take a turn reading a sentence of the crazy tale that has developed. Here's an example of a fill-in-the-blank tale about how the bride and groom met.

(Bride's name) and (groom's name) were standing near each other at a club when their (body part—plural) first touched. She was wearing a (color) (article of clothing) and nothing else. He (verb—past tense) and she felt her heart skip a beat.

He introduced himself, saying his name was (groom's name) but that his friends called him (nickname). She understood right away because she could tell he had a (size) (noun). She had never seen one quite like that before.

He asked her if she would like to (verb) sometime. She said she would love to. The two exchanged phone numbers, but that's not all. (Groom's name) also gave (bride's name) a (noun). Right away she knew it was the (adjective ending in "est") she had ever had. The two made (adjective) (noun) and (verb—past tense) the night away.

Over the next few months, the two (verb—past tense) a lot and soon (groom's name) felt it was time to ask her to (verb) him. He popped the (noun) and she said (exclamation). After all, she knew she had found the (noun) of her dreams.

Hungman

Here's the bachelorette version of hangman. Select several phrases having to do with love, sex, or marriage. Draw lines on a piece of poster board that represent the letters of each word in the first phrase. Include spaces between words as required. For example, you might use "Is that a Tic Tac in your pocket or are you just happy to see me?" Have guests take turns guessing letters that might be found in the phrase. If a bachelorette guesses correctly, the letter is written on the appropriate line(s) and she guesses again. If she selects a letter not found in the phrase, she must draw a body part on her hungman on the hanging post. Make copies of the blank game sheet on page 121. A bachelorette can no longer guess letters once she has completed her hungman. Award a point to the guest who guesses the entire phrase correctly, then move to the next phrase. The guest with the most points wins. Required body parts might include the following:

- Head
- Torso
- Two arms
- Two legs
- Male anatomy

Prizes

You'll have lots of fun shopping for game prizes. Spend time browsing in an adult novelty store and also consider the following:

- Subscription to *Playgirl*
- Large summer sausage
- Bag of green M&Ms, can of oysters, or other aphrodisiacs
- Sexy lingerie
- Massage oil
- Adult video or book
- Novelty condoms
- Tickets to a male revue
- Sex toys
- Hangover remedies (such as a sponge to soak up all the alcohol)

Many of the favor ideas starting on page 101 can double as game prizes.

Drinking Games

Please review the transportation and location solutions outlined in Chapter 1 and make responsible decisions if your plans involve alcohol. If planning at party at home, Chapter 5 contains lots of fun drink recipes that include many nonalcoholic options.

Blow Job

Have bachelorettes stand in a circle. Inflate a condom like a balloon and begin bouncing it around the circle without letting it drop to the floor. Whoever lets it drop has to take a drink. You could also use a feather instead of an inflated condom.

Rhyming Charades

Divide guests into two teams. Have team one leave the room to think of a secret word having to do with love, sex, or marriage. They must also think of rhyming words. When they're ready, have them return and act out the words that rhyme with the secret word. Team two tries to guess the rhyming words and eventually guess the secret word. For example, if the secret word is *marry*, team one might act out *fairy*, *carry*, *scary*, and so on. If team two fails to identify the secret word within the time limit, they have to drink. Take turns acting out rhyming words.

The Who Game

If your bachelorette party is scheduled during the holiday season, then watching *How the Grinch Stole Christmas* would be fun, especially if guests had to take a drink each time the word *grinch* was mentioned. This game could be played any time of year with popular movies or TV classics like *Happy Days*, in which guests would toast whenever they saw the gang at Arnold's or whenever someone said, "Fonzie."

Categories

This perennial favorite can easily be adapted into a drinking game. Bachelorettes take turns thinking of categories having to do with love, sex, or marriage. Once a category is established, each bachelorette lists an item contained within that category. For example, in the category "famous brides," Princess Diana would be a good choice. Other categories might include old boyfriends, honeymoon destinations, eligible bachelors, movies that include a wedding, and so on. When someone comes up empty for either a category or an item within a category, she must drink. A time limit should be established before play begins.

The Name Game

Have bachelorettes sit in a circle. Let the bride get things started by saying the name of a famous person. The bachelorette to her right should follow with a famous person's name that starts with the first letter of the last name of the bride's famous person. It continues from there. For example, if the bride says, "Joe DiMaggio," the bachelorette who follows her could say, "David Letterman." If she says a name that uses the letter D in both the first and last names, such as Danny Devito, then the play reverses direction. The same thing happens if a bachelorette thinks of a famous person who goes by only one name, such as Cher. Anyone who can't come up with an answer in the allotted time has to drink.

Blow Me

Place a deck of cards on top of an empty beer bottle. The object of the game is to blow the cards off the bottle. If only one card falls off, the blower drinks alone. If more than one falls off, everyone drinks. If someone blows off all the cards, they have to drink continuously while the rest of the group sings, "Here's to sister (blower's name), sister (name), sister (name). Oh, here's to sister (name) who's with us tonight." The group can pick an appropriate tune. Make up variations such as if a joker appears, the person to the blower's left does a shot.

Taboo

Before the party gets underway, make a rule that certain words will be off limits during the evening's festivities. For example, declare that no one can mention the groom's name or the words *wedding, beer,* and so on the entire evening. If someone says a forbidden word, she must do a shot. You might also choose to make certain actions off limits, such as drinking with your right hand.

Variation: Play with condoms instead of drinks. At the beginning of the party, give each guest ten condoms. Each time a guest uses a taboo word, she must forfeit a condom to the person who catches her. The guest who collects the most condoms wins a prize.

Old Lush

Drag out the Old Maid deck and let the fun begin. This time the Old Maid card will be an Old Lush card. Bachelorettes must swig every time a card is drawn that does not produce a matching pair. Whoever is left with the Old Lush gets to tell someone to do a shot.

THE BLUSHING BRIDE

This is your special chance to spotlight the bride, so don't be afraid to let it all hang out. However, make sure you select ideas that fit well with her personality. If she's willing, you might adorn her with an eye-catching train made of condoms, or challenge her to complete a hysterical and embarrassing set of tasks. Whatever you decide, don't forget your camera.

Creative Bridal Attire

Of course you'll want to make sure the bride is appropriately dressed for the occasion. Consider tying wedding bells to her shoes so she won't go unnoticed, or create a more elaborate fashion statement from the ideas that follow.

Funny Condom Veil

Supplies:
- 5 nonlubricated condoms
- Headband
- 1 yard white tulle
- Glue gun
- Bridal trims

Directions: Gather tulle and glue to headband. Embellish with condoms and other bridal trims.

Variation: Blow up condoms like balloons. Space evenly along headband and tie to secure. Glue tulle to underside of headband to form veil. Embellish with bridal trims.

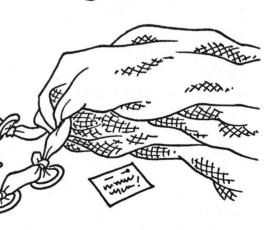

Rubber-Made Train

Supplies:
- Nonlubricated condoms (about 10 for a size 8 bride)
- 3⅓ yards white tulle
- Paper
- Markers
- Straight pins

Directions: Tie condoms end to end to form belt for bride's waist. Fold tulle in half lengthwise. Drape over belt and tie belt at bride's waist with tulle hanging in back. Pin funny sayings to train such as, "I'm tying the knot, so buy me a shot."

Colorful Condom Corsage

Supplies:
- 3 nonlubricated condoms
- Curling ribbon in various bright colors
- Scissors

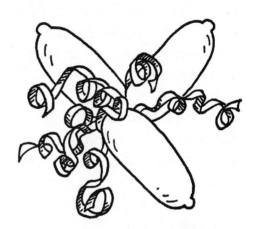

Directions: Partially inflate condoms. Tie together with ribbons and curl with scissors.

Shopping Spree

Take the bride out to buy the most outrageous outfit she can find—one she would never dream of wearing with her fiancé. Take up a collection among bachelorettes to finance the party clothes. To complete her look, arrange for a free makeover at a department store, a new hairstyle for the evening, a manicure, and anything else to pamper her from head to toe.

Bridal Plunger

Since your dear friend is about to take the plunge, decorate a plunger for her to carry as a scepter on your bachelorette escapades. Paint the plunger white, decorate it with a tulle bow, and glue a small bride-and-groom cake topper to the top of the handle.

Bachelor-et-a-Kit

This kit features everything you need to make the bride blush including a veil, flashing ring, T-shirt, bridal garter, boa, personalized fairy tale, and instructions for a bachelorette scavenger hunt. Call the distributor toll-free at 888-438-6548 for more details, or visit it online at www.etakit.com.

Marry-Making Bridal Escapades

These games will guarantee that the soon-to-be-wed will not soon forget her special evening.

Design-Her-a-Gown

Here's a lighthearted game of revenge and the perfect activity if most of the bridesmaids will be attending the bachelorette party. Since the bride gets to pick out the bridesmaids' dresses for the wedding, the brides-maids should get to pick out the bride's dress for the bachelorette party. Bridesmaids can create a bridal gown and veil from a variety of creative materials including tulle, ribbon, lace, flowers, and unexpected items such as condoms and toilet paper. The better the prop box, the more outlandish the attire.

Bridal Quest

This activity challenges the bride to a series of hilarious stunts designed by the bachelorettes. Have each guest write down a daring feat for the bride to complete during the evening. The pictures will be priceless. Consider the following:

- Kissing a bald guy
- Finding a guy to fashion a bridal train from toilet paper
- Spoon-feeding a Jell-O shot to a strange guy (page 88)
- Finding a guy who has more body piercings than you
- Securing a wallet-sized photo of a stranger's wife or girlfriend
- Obtaining a man's chest hair
- Dancing with a guy who has the same name as the groom
- Getting a guy to give up his underwear
- Collecting a dozen business cards from strange men
- Offering to give a guy a Blow Job—the shot, that is (page 87)
- Obtaining a condom from a stranger
- Finding a guy to buy each bachelorette a drink

Variation: Write the bride's tasks on slips of paper. Insert them into condoms and inflate. Secure the condoms with ribbons and have the bride carry a balloon bouquet. Burst a balloon at each stop and have the bride perform the enclosed task.

Suck for a Buck

If you're looking for an easy activity that will provide loads of laughs, this *fun*draiser may be just what you're looking for. It requires sewing candy pieces all over a T-shirt or sash. The bride must wear the garment the night of the party, and gentlemen are invited to chew off a piece of candy for a dollar.

Variation #1: A similar game is called "Blow for a Buck," in which bubble gum replaces candy.
Variation #2: Provide the bride and bachelorettes with candy necklaces. Invite guys to eat a piece of candy for a buck. The first one to get rid of all her candy wins.

The Name Game

Write several guys' names on a T-shirt. Have the bride wear the shirt the night of the party. During the festivities, have her look for guys whose names appear on the shirt. When she finds one, have her ask him to sign the shirt by his name. At designated intervals throughout the evening, have her do a shot if she still has names without signatures. Be sure to include a few uncommon names.

EAT, DRINK, AND BE MARRIED

Here you'll find delicious recipes to spice up your party and tantalize your bachelorettes' taste buds. Design a menu that's uniquely your own. Make sure to offer a wide variety of flavors, textures, colors, temperatures, and low-calorie options. Remember to consider the amount of available refrigerator and freezer space, and avoid serving too many dishes that require last-minute attention. A make-ahead menu will lighten your load as hostess.

The following tips and no-fuss recipes are designed to help you wine and dine your bachelorettes without a lot of time spent in the kitchen. After all, you want to enjoy the party, too!

Appetizers

When planning your menu, consider that the longer the party will be, the heartier the appetizers should be. If you're not planning to serve dinner at all, then figure on a minimum of ten appetizers per guest.

Remember that alcohol can sometimes induce mild to severe cases of the munchies. A well-prepared hostess will have plenty of reinforcements ready to go if this type of outbreak occurs. Consider serving appetizers with personalized picks made by gluing small photo cutouts of the bride to toothpicks.

A Big 10-Inch

1 loaf frozen bread dough, thawed
8-ounce package sliced pepperoni
8-ounce package shredded mozzarella cheese
1 teaspoon garlic powder
1 egg white
1 teaspoon water

Preheat oven to 350°F. Roll out thawed bread dough to approximately 10-by-12-inch size. Cover bread with pepperoni slices and sprinkle with cheese and garlic powder. Roll up very tightly and tuck in ends. Place seam side down on a greased cookie sheet. Brush with egg glaze (1 egg white whipped with 1 teaspoon water) and bake for 25 minutes or until golden brown. You'll know it's ready if it sounds hollow when thumped.

Chicken Strips with Sweet Sauce

Chicken: 6 boneless chicken breasts
½ cup pineapple juice
¼ cup olive oil
¼ cup apple juice
2 tablespoons soy sauce

Cut chicken breasts into strips. Place in glass baking dish. Mix remaining ingredients and pour over chicken. Marinate in refrigerator for at least 6 hours. Preheat oven to broil. Cook chicken for 10 minutes or until done. Serve hot or cold with the following sweet sauce.

Sweet Sauce: 2 mangos, peeled and chopped
3 tablespoons honey
¼ cup lime juice

Mix all ingredients in blender until smooth. *Yield: 2 cups*

Cocktail Meatballs

Meatballs: 3 pounds hamburger
2 cups oatmeal
2 eggs
2 tablespoons minced onion
2 tablespoons chili powder
2 teaspoons salt
1 teaspoon garlic powder
1 teaspoon pepper

Sauce: 2 cups ketchup
1½ cups brown sugar
¼ cup minced onion
2 tablespoons liquid smoke
½ teaspoon garlic powder

Preheat oven to 300°F. Mix meatball ingredients and form into balls. Brown in nonstick skillet and place in casserole dish. Mix sauce ingredients and pour over meatballs. Bake for 40 minutes or until cooked thoroughly.
Yield: 45 2-inch meatballs

Crab Yummies

1 stick butter, softened
5-ounce jar Old English cheese spread
1½ teaspoons mayonnaise
½ teaspoon garlic powder
6-ounce can crabmeat, drained
6 English muffins

Preheat oven to 350°F. Mix first 4 ingredients. Stir in crabmeat and spread on split muffins. Cut muffins into quarters. Place on cookie sheet and freeze for 10 minutes. Remove and bake for 10 minutes until hot and bubbly.

Hey Cheese Ball I

2 8-ounce packages cream cheese
8-ounce can crushed pineapple, drained
¼ cup green pepper, chopped
2 tablespoons green onion, chopped
2 teaspoons seasoned salt
2 cups chopped nuts

Use fork to mix all ingredients well, except 1 cup of nuts. Sprinkle remaining cup of nuts onto plastic wrap. Mold cheese mixture into desired shape and roll in nuts. Wrap in plastic and refrigerate overnight. Serve with crackers.

Hey Cheese Ball II

2 8-ounce packages cream cheese
8-ounce package finely shredded cheddar cheese
⅔ cup green pepper, chopped
¼ cup margarine
¼ cup green onion, chopped
2 teaspoons soy sauce
1 teaspoon lemon juice
1 cup chopped nuts

Use fork to mix all ingredients well, except nuts. Sprinkle nuts onto plastic wrap. Mold cheese mixture into desired shape and roll in nuts. Wrap in plastic and refrigerate overnight. Serve with crackers.

Party Pinwheels

1 cup sour cream
8-ounce package cream cheese, softened
4.5-ounce can chopped green chiles, drained
1 cup finely shredded cheddar cheese
½ cup green onion, chopped
4.25-ounce can chopped black olives, drained
5 10-inch flour tortillas
dash garlic salt

Mix first six ingredients and spread evenly on tortillas. Sprinkle with garlic salt and roll tortillas into cylinders. Wrap cylinders in plastic wrap, place in refrigerator, and allow mixture to set. Remove and slice into pinwheels with sharp knife. Serve with salsa and sour cream. *Yield: 45 ½-inch pinwheels*

Pasta Salad

(Try this recipe with novelty-shaped pasta. To order, call The Pasta Shoppe at 800-247-0188.)

¾ cup sugar
¾ cup white vinegar
½ cup vegetable oil
2 tablespoons mustard
1 tablespoon garlic salt
1 tablespoon parsley flakes
1 tablespoon dill weed
1 tablespoon Accent
¼ teaspoon pepper
12-ounce package spiral or novelty-shaped pasta, cooked

Mix all ingredients except pasta. Pour mixture over cooked pasta and fold in gently. The secret is not to leave out any of the ingredients. You can also toss in bacon bits, cheese squares, or chopped veggies such as cucumber, onion, green pepper, or tomato. Refrigerate for several hours before serving to allow flavors to blend. *Yield: 6 2-ounce servings*

Pretzel Dip-Sticks with Honey Mustard Sauce

Pretzels: 2 10-ounce cans refrigerated pizza crust
2 eggs
1 teaspoon salt
2 tablespoons coarse salt

Preheat oven to 425°F. Unroll pizza dough and cut into 1-inch strips. Twist and place on greased cookie sheet. Brush strips with egg and salt mixture. Sprinkle with coarse salt. Bake for 10 minutes or until golden. Serve with honey mustard sauce. *Yield: 18 dip-sticks*

Sauce: ¾ cup mayonnaise
3 tablespoons Dijon mustard
3 tablespoons honey

Mix ingredients and serve with pretzels or chicken strips. *Yield: 1 cup*

Sweetart Franks

10-ounce jar grape jelly
20-ounce can chili sauce
2 pounds cocktail wieners

Heat jelly and chili sauce in crock pot. Add wieners and simmer for 1 hour.

Dips

Here's the skinny on more than a dozen yummy dips. Whatever your tastes, these tried and true recipes are guaranteed hits for any hostess. Present your dips in appetizing containers for an even more enjoyable experience. Several of the following recipes recommend serving in hollowed-out loaves of bread, but the fun shouldn't stop there. You can serve individual portions in hollowed-out bread rolls or vegetables. A slice of pineapple might be the perfect canvas for individual fruit dips. If serving as an appetizer, plan on two cups of dip for eight people.

A Big Schlong of Clam Dip

16-ounce loaf Italian bread
8-ounce package herb-flavored cream cheese, softened
8-ounce package plain cream cheese, softened
3 8-ounce cans minced clams (Drain 2 cans.)
3 tablespoons lemon juice
¼ cup dried parsley flakes
2 tablespoons Worcestershire sauce
1 teaspoon minced onion
2 drops Tabasco sauce
¼ teaspoon salt
¼ teaspoon ground pepper

Preheat oven to 350°F. Cut top off bread and remove the insides to form bowl. Save bread pieces for dipping. Mix all other ingredients including 1 can clam juice. Transfer mixture into hollowed-out bread loaf and replace bread top. Wrap bread in foil and bake for 3 hours. Carefully remove foil and place bread on serving tray. Creatively garnish by placing 2 cheese balls at one end of loaf. Cheese ball recipes start on page 58. Serve with bread pieces, crackers, or veggies. *Yield: 4 cups*

Crab Rangoon Dip

2 8-ounce packages cream cheese, softened
½ cup sour cream
2 tablespoons powdered sugar
1½ teaspoons Worcestershire sauce
½ teaspoon lemon juice
¼ teaspoon garlic powder
2 6-ounce cans crabmeat, drained
2 tablespoons green onion, chopped

Mix all ingredients, adding crabmeat and green onion last. Refrigerate until ready to serve. Serve with strips from your favorite Chinese restaurant or make your own by cutting egg roll wrappers into ¾-inch strips and deep frying. *Yield: 5 cups*

Goes-Good-with-Beer Chipped Beef Dip

3 8-ounce packages cream cheese, softened
10.75-ounce can cream of mushroom soup
1 tablespoon minced onion
1 teaspoon lemon juice
2 2.5-ounce packages dried beef

Mix the first 4 ingredients together. Cut dried beef into small pieces and add to mixture. Refrigerate several hours before serving with chips, Fritos, crackers, or veggies. *Yield: 5 cups*

Hot Bacon Cheese Spread

16-ounce loaf round bread
12 slices crisp bacon, crumbled
8-ounce package shredded Colby or Monterey Jack cheese
1 cup grated Parmesan cheese
1 cup mayonnaise
½ cup green onion, chopped
1 clove garlic, minced

Preheat oven to 350°F. Slice top off bread and remove center to form bowl. Blend remaining ingredients in mixing bowl. Transfer mixture to bread bowl. Replace top on bread bowl and bake on cookie sheet for one hour. Serve with bread pieces, bacon breadsticks (page 68), pita bits (page 69), or bagel chips (page 69). *Yield: 3 cups*

Mexican Dip

2 8-ounce packages cream cheese, softened
¼ cup green pepper, diced (Save other half of pepper for garnish.)
2.25-ounce can sliced black olives, drained
11.5-ounce jar salsa
8-ounce package shredded mozzarella cheese
8-ounce package shredded cheddar cheese

Spread cream cheese as base onto bottom of shallow dish with lip. Mix green pepper, black olives, and salsa together and add to top of cream cheese. Sprinkle with shredded cheeses. For garnish, cut novelty shapes from green pepper using cookie cutters. Line the edges of serving dish with tortilla chips.

Pizza-in-a-Jiffy Dip

8-ounce package cream cheese, softened
1 teaspoon Italian seasoning
8-ounce package shredded mozzarella cheese
½ cup pizza sauce
⅓ cup pepperoni, chopped
2 tablespoons green pepper, chopped

Preheat oven to 350°F. Mix cream cheese with Italian seasoning and spread on bottom of 9-inch pie pan. Add the following layers: 1 cup mozzarella cheese, pizza sauce, another cup mozzarella cheese, chopped pepperoni, and green pepper. Bake 20 minutes or until cheese is melted. Serve with breadsticks or slices of French bread.

Spinach Artichoke Dip

10-ounce box frozen spinach, thawed and drained
1⅛ cups grated Parmesan cheese
4 ounces cream cheese, softened
1 cup mayonnaise
14-ounce can artichokes, chopped and drained
1 tablespoon green onion, chopped
1 clove garlic, minced
1 teaspoon paprika

Preheat oven to 350°F. Mix all ingredients except for ⅛ cup Parmesan cheese and paprika. Place in greased 8-inch-square casserole dish. Top with remaining Parmesan cheese and paprika. Bake 25 minutes. Serve with tortilla chips, salsa, and sour cream.

Wine and Cheese Fondue

1 clove garlic
1 cup dry white wine
1½ cups grated cheese (Try an herb or garlic variety.)
1½ cups grated Swiss cheese
2 tablespoons flour

Cut clove of garlic in half and rub on inside of saucepan to flavor. Add wine to saucepan and heat. In bowl, toss cheeses with flour to coat. When wine becomes hot, add small amounts of cheese mixture, stirring constantly. Transfer to fondue pot and serve with slices of French bread.
Yield: 2 cups

Kahlua Fruit Dip

1 cup sour cream
4 ounces cream cheese, softened
¼ cup powdered sugar
¼ cup Kahlua

Blend ingredients with whisk or mixer. Refrigerate 2 hours. Serve with fresh fruit and cookies. *Yield: 1½ cups*

Tropical Fruit Dip

8-ounce can crushed pineapple
3.4-ounce package instant coconut creme pudding mix
¾ cup milk
½ cup sour cream
1 teaspoon poppy seeds

Mix all ingredients in blender for 1 minute. Refrigerate several hours to allow flavors to blend. Serve with fresh fruit and cookies. *Yield: 2 cups*

Chocoholic's Fondue

12 1-ounce semisweet baking chocolate squares
¾ cup heavy cream
2 tablespoons brandy
1 tablespoon butter

Slowly melt chocolate over low heat in heavy saucepan. Stir in cream, brandy, and butter. Serve in small crock to keep warm or use fondue pot. Be careful not to let chocolate boil. Serve with fresh fruit, cookies, or angel food cake. *Yield: 2 cups*

Virgin Chocolate Fondue

6-ounce bar white chocolate
½ cup miniature marshmallows
¼ cup whipping cream
2 tablespoons butter

Break chocolate into small pieces. Melt all ingredients over low heat in saucepan. Serve with fresh fruit. *Yield: 1 cup*

Munchies

Many of the recipes that follow work well on their own or with dips. Remember, the saltier the snacks, the more drinks you'll need.

Bacon Breadsticks

1 pound bacon, sliced
3.25-ounce package thin breadsticks
⅔ cup grated Parmesan cheese

Preheat oven to 250°F. Wrap bacon slices around breadsticks. Sprinkle with Parmesan cheese and bake on greased cookie sheet for 1 hour. *Yield: 22 breadsticks*

Bagel Chips

For each bagel: 1 tablespoon vegetable oil
                    1 tablespoon grated Parmesan cheese
                    ½ teaspoon garlic salt

Preheat oven to 325°F. Slice bagel to form small discs. Brush bagel slices with oil. Sprinkle with Parmesan cheese and garlic salt. Place on cookie sheet and bake for 10 minutes.

Baked Pita Bits

For each 6-inch pita: 2 tablespoons olive oil
                        dash garlic salt

Preheat oven to 375°F. Split pita in half. Cover each half with 1 table-spoon olive oil and a dash of garlic salt. Slice pita into wedges and bake until crisp.

Barbecued Nuts

4 cups roasted salted mixed nuts
⅛ cup spicy barbecue sauce
2½ tablespoons grated Parmesan cheese

Preheat oven to 300°F. In bowl, cover nuts with barbecue sauce and stir. Place on cookie sheet and sprinkle with Parmesan cheese. Bake for 20 minutes. Remove and place on wax paper to cool. Store in airtight container until serving. *Yield: 4 cups*

Chocolate-Covered Nutty Popcorn

1 bag microwave popcorn, popped (Remove hulls.)
½ cup cashews
½ cup honey roasted peanuts
2 7-ounce Hershey's milk chocolate bars with almonds

Break chocolate bars into pieces and melt on low in microwave. Mix popcorn and nuts on baking sheet covered with wax paper. Coat popcorn and nut mixture with melted chocolate. Cool and store in airtight container until serving. *Yield: 12 cups*

Horny Party Mix

1 pound green M&Ms
5 cups Crispix
5 cups Cheerios
2 cups salted peanuts
12-ounce bag pretzel twists
2 12-ounce packages white chocolate
3 tablespoons vegetable oil

Mix first five ingredients on wax paper. Microwave white chocolate and oil on high for 2 minutes. Drizzle mixture over other ingredients and let cool on wax paper. Store in airtight container until serving. *Yield: 20 cups*

Desserts and Other Aphrodisiacs

Here are some orgasmic desserts sure to tempt any bachelorette.

A Berry Chocolate Brownie
1 cup unsalted butter
5 ounces unsweetened chocolate
2 cups sugar
4 large eggs
2 teaspoons vanilla extract
1¼ cups flour
1 teaspoon baking powder
½ teaspoon salt
1 cup chopped walnuts
10-ounce jar raspberry jam

Preheat oven to 350°F. Melt butter and chocolate together over low heat. Pour mixture into bowl and stir in other ingredients except for jam. Put half of the mixture in a greased 11½-by-8-inch pan. Set in freezer for 15 minutes. Remove and spread with a thin layer of raspberry jam. Add remaining chocolate batter and let set until mixture becomes room temperature. Bake for 40 minutes and cool. Slice and serve. If desired, garnish sliced brownies with fresh raspberries.

Beefcake

To form your cut-out Beefcake, you'll need to bake one 13-by-9-inch cake and one 9-inch round cake. Use your favorite recipe or try the following for a basic white 13-by-9-inch cake. Cut the same recipe in half to make the 9-inch round cake.

2¼ cups flour
1 tablespoon baking powder
½ teaspoon salt
1⅜ cups sugar
¼ cup margarine, softened
1 cup milk
2 teaspoons vanilla extract
3 egg whites

Preheat oven to 350°F. Sift flour and baking powder into mixing bowl. Add salt, sugar, margarine, milk, vanilla, and egg whites. Blend until smooth. Pour into greased cake pan lined with wax paper and bake for 35 minutes. Allow cake to cool before removing from pan.

To form cutout, wrap cake in plastic and freeze for 30 minutes (for easier cutting and fewer crumbs). Remove from freezer and cut according to the following diagram.

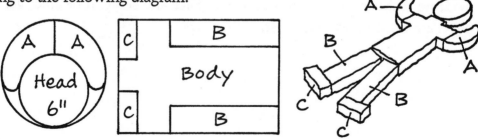

Place cake on sturdy piece of cardboard covered with foil. Decorate with skin-colored icing, except for boxer shorts. Use brown M&Ms for eyes, orange gumdrop for nose, red fruit slice cut in half for mouth, pink Necco wafers for cheeks, and butterscotch chips for nipples on chest. Toast coconut and use as hair. To toast coconut, place in shallow baking dish in oven at 350°F for 8 minutes, stirring occasionally until lightly browned. Cover most of body with toasted coconut to transform Beefcake into Hairy Hal. Complete your male anatomy with a Twinkie. Add a funny conversation bubble if Beefcake has something to say to the bride. Or, add a dumbbell by icing 2 cupcakes and placing a piece of licorice between them.

Better-Than-Sex Cake
1 chocolate cake, from scratch or box
14-ounce can sweetened condensed milk
12.25-ounce jar butterscotch topping
12-ounce container whipped topping
3 1.4-ounce Heath bars, crushed

Bake a 13-by-9-inch chocolate cake according to directions. Remove cake from oven and randomly poke holes in cake top with end of wooden spoon handle while cake is still warm. Combine condensed milk and butterscotch topping. Pour over cake top. Let cool. Ice cake with whipped topping. Sprinkle with Heath bar crumbs. Freeze overnight and serve.

Butterscotch Cheesecake Bars

11-ounce package butterscotch chips
1 stick butter
2 cups graham cracker crumbs
1 cup chopped pecans
8-ounce package cream cheese, softened
14-ounce can sweetened condensed milk
1 teaspoon vanilla extract
1 egg

Preheat oven to 325°F. Grease 13-by-9-inch pan. Melt butterscotch chips and butter in saucepan. Stir in graham cracker crumbs and pecans. Press half of mixture into pan. Beat cream cheese in mixing bowl until fluffy. Stir in condensed milk, vanilla, and egg. Pour over crust in pan. Top with remaining half of crumb mixture. Bake 30 minutes. Cut while warm. Refrigerate until serving.

Champagne Sherbet

1 quart lemon sherbet
½ pint raspberry sherbet
1 cup pink champagne

Place sherbets in large bowl to soften. Mix sherbets together and add ½ cup pink champagne. Place mixture into individual plastic parfait glasses and freeze. Top with remaining champagne and serve with assorted cookies. *Yield: 8 6-ounce servings*

Ice Cream Gift Package

Place half-gallon block of your favorite ice cream on serving platter. Press 18 Vienna fingers sandwich cookies around the edges of ice cream. Tie decorative wired ribbon around cookies to secure in place. Freeze until firm. Top with whipped topping and garnish with sprinkles, cherries, or candy conversation hearts.

Kahlua Cake

For cake:　　18.25-ounce box yellow cake mix
3.9-ounce box instant chocolate pudding mix
1 cup vegetable oil
4 eggs
¾ cup water
¼ cup Kahlua
¼ cup vodka

For topping:　¼ cup Kahlua
½ cup powdered sugar

Preheat oven to 350°F. Blend all cake ingredients until smooth. Pour into greased bundt pan. Bake for 45 minutes. Cool before removing from pan. Top with Kahlua followed by powdered sugar.

Oohey Gooey Buttercakes

18.5-ounce box butter recipe yellow cake mix
4 eggs
1 stick butter, melted
8-ounce package cream cheese, softened
1 teaspoon vanilla extract
1½ cups powdered sugar

Preheat oven to 350°F. Stir together cake mix, 2 eggs, and butter. Pat mixture into bottom of greased 13-by-9-inch pan. Mix cream cheese, 2 eggs, vanilla, and powdered sugar. Spread cream cheese mixture over cake batter. Bake for 40 minutes. Allow to cool and cut into bars. *Tip*: You could bake and freeze ahead of time. Serve cold or at room temperature.

Piña Colada Cake

For cake: 18.25-ounce box yellow cake mix
1 cup water
½ cup vegetable oil
1 teaspoon rum extract
1 teaspoon coconut extract
3 eggs

For topping: 3.4-ounce box instant vanilla pudding mix
⅔ cup bottled piña colada mix
8-ounce can crushed pineapple, drained
1 cup whipping cream, whipped
¼ cup toasted* coconut
paper umbrellas

Preheat oven to 350°F. Blend all cake ingredients until smooth. Pour into greased 13-by-9-inch pan. Bake for 30 minutes or until done. Cool completely. For topping, combine pudding and piña colada mixes with pineapple. Fold in whipping cream and spread over cake. Top with toasted coconut. Refrigerate several hours before serving. Garnish with paper umbrellas.

*To toast coconut, bake in shallow pan at 350°F for 8 minutes, stirring occasionally until lightly browned.

Sex in a Pan
1 cup flour
1 stick butter, softened
8-ounce package cream cheese, softened
¼ cup powdered sugar
16-ounce container whipped topping
2 3.9-ounce boxes instant chocolate pudding mix
1 cup milk

Preheat oven to 375°F. Mix flour and butter. Press mixture on bottom of greased 8-inch-square pan. Bake for 10 minutes. Let cool. Mix together cream cheese and powdered sugar with approximately 8 ounces of whipped topping. Spread mixture on cooled crust. Blend chocolate pudding mix with milk and layer. Add remaining whipped topping as finishing touch. Refrigerate until serving.

Uniquely Shaped Sugar Cookies

18-ounce package refrigerated sugar cookie dough
flour

Preheat oven to 350°F. Remove dough from package. Cut dough in half. Wrap one half in plastic wrap and return to refrigerator. Roll other half on floured surface to ¼-inch thickness. Use flour as needed to reduce stickiness. Cut out desired cookie shapes. (See instructions that follow.) Place on greased cookie sheet and bake for 10 minutes or until edges turn golden. Remove and cool on wire racks. Repeat process with other half of dough.

To cut unique cookie patterns, place wax paper over template and trace with pencil. Cut out design. Tape cutout to lightweight cardboard and cut along outline with scissors. Place cardboard pattern on cookie dough and cut around pattern with paring knife. You'll find a bachelorette cookie template on page 119.

Who-Took-My-Cherry Dessert

20-ounce can cherry pie filling
18.25-ounce box white cake mix
½ cup crushed walnuts
1 stick margarine, melted

Preheat oven to 350°F. Pour cherry pie filling into lightly greased 9-inch-square baking dish. Cover with cake mix and top with crushed walnuts. Pour melted butter over top. Bake for 30 minutes and serve.

Punch

Here are some recipes that really pack a punch. For added pleasure, use a carved-out watermelon as your serving bowl or toss a few condoms into your ice ring before freezing—they'll float in the punch once the ring melts. For best results, use the same juice from the recipe in your ice ring to avoid diluting your punch.

Berry Good Champagne Punch
3-ounce package berry gelatin
1 cup boiling water
6-ounce can frozen lemonade concentrate, thawed
2 cups cold water
750-ml bottle rosé wine, chilled
750-ml bottle champagne, chilled
2 cups fresh strawberries, frozen*

Dissolve gelatin in boiling water. After gelatin mixture cools, mix in punch bowl with lemonade concentrate and cold water. Add wine, champagne, and frozen strawberries just before serving.

*Wash strawberries, remove stems, and dry. Place in plastic bag and freeze. The frozen strawberries will have both a beautiful and chilling effect on the punch. *Yield: 1 gallon*

Daiquiri Lush Slush

1 cup sugar
4 cups water
12-ounce can frozen lemonade concentrate, thawed
12-ounce can frozen limeade concentrate, thawed
1 cup light rum
2-liter bottle ginger ale

Boil sugar and water for 5 minutes, then cool. Combine sugar-and-water mixture with all ingredients except ginger ale in large plastic container. Cover and freeze. Remove approximately 30 minutes before serving. Place frozen mixture in punch bowl. Add ginger ale and stir just before serving. *Yield: 1 gallon*

Designated Driver Champagne Punch

46-ounce can white grape juice
1-liter bottle club soda
2 24-ounce bottles lemon-lime soda

Mix all ingredients and serve chilled. *Yield: 1 gallon*

Let's-Monkey-Around Punch

5 bananas
46-ounce can pineapple juice
12-ounce can frozen orange juice concentrate, slightly thawed
12-ounce can frozen lemonade concentrate, slightly thawed
2 cups sugar
3 cups water
2 2-liter bottles lemon-lime soda, chilled

Place peeled bananas in blender. Add enough pineapple juice to cover and blend with orange juice and lemonade concentrates. Pour contents into a one-gallon container. Stir in sugar, water, and rest of pineapple juice. Freeze. Remove container from freezer a few hours before the party so the mixture can thaw slightly before serving. Transfer to two-gallon punch bowl and pour on lemon-lime soda. *Yield: 1½ gallons*

Rum Punch

36 ounces orange juice
46-ounce can pineapple juice
12 ounces gold rum
12 ounces coconut rum
6 ounces apricot brandy

Mix ingredients. Serve over generous amounts of ice in individual glasses. *Yield: 1 gallon*

Frozen Froo-Froos

Rev up your blenders. Here are the recipes favored among bachelorettes but dreaded by busy bartenders everywhere. Each recipe is designed to make one blender full. Don't forget the Crazy Straws on page 94.

Berry Buzz

12-ounce can frozen orange juice concentrate, thawed
12-ounce can frozen lemonade concentrate, thawed
2 cups water
2 cups prepared iced tea
1 cup sugar
1½ cups vodka
20-ounce package strawberries with sugar, frozen

Mix ingredients in blender and freeze the day before the party. Remove one hour before party. Serve in chilled cocktail glasses.

Blue Hawaiian

8 ounces pineapple juice
4 ounces blue curacao
4 ounces coconut rum

Mix ingredients in blender with ice until slushy. Serve in chilled cocktail glasses.

Fudgesicle

3 ounces chocolate syrup
5 scoops vanilla ice cream
1 ounce amaretto
4 ounces rum 151
1 banana, sliced

Mix ingredients in blender with ice until slushy. Serve in chilled cocktail glasses.

Margarita Brain Freeze

4 ounces tequila
4 ounces lime juice
2 ounces triple sec

Mix ingredients in blender with ice until slushy. Rub glass rims with lime wedge, then dip each glass in saucer of coarse salt.

Virgin Margaritas

6-ounce can frozen lemonade concentrate
6-ounce can frozen limeade concentrate
¼ cup powdered sugar
20 ounces club soda, chilled

Mix ingredients in blender with ice until slushy. Rub glass rims with lime wedge, then dip each glass in saucer of sugar.

Piña Colada

2 cups piña colada mix
4 ounces coconut cream
3 ounces pineapple juice
2 ounces light rum

Mix ingredients in blender with ice until slushy. Blend until smooth.
Serve in chilled cocktail glasses and garnish with pineapple.

Protein Shake

9 ounces pineapple juice
1½ ounces coconut rum
1½ ounces piña colada mix
1½ ounces peach schnapps
1½ ounces banana liqueur

Mix ingredients in blender with ice until slushy. Serve in chilled cocktail
glasses.

Teetotalers Creamy Cranberry Cocktail

5 ounces cranberry juice
4 ounces apple juice
1 ounce coconut cream
1 ounce lime juice
2 teaspoons grenadine

Mix ingredients in blender with ice until slushy. Serve in chilled cocktail
glasses.

Cocktails and Mocktails

If you don't currently feature *bartender* on your résumé, you'll soon be adding it after wowing your guests with the following concoctions.

Caribbean Champagne

light rum
banana liqueur
750-ml bottle champagne, chilled

Pour ½ teaspoon of both light rum and banana liqueur into each chilled champagne glass. Fill glasses with champagne and stir. For a nonalcoholic version, substitute pineapple juice for champagne.

Get *Lei-d*

4 ounces pineapple juice
½ ounce cranberry juice
¾ ounce vodka
¾ ounce raspberry schnapps

Mix ingredients in cocktail shaker. Serve over ice in chilled cocktail glasses.

Just Peachy

peach schnapps
750-ml bottle champagne, chilled

Fill each chilled champagne glass with one-fourth peach schnapps and three-fourths champagne. Stir and serve.

Pink Sweetarts

64 ounces lemonade made from 12-ounce can frozen concentrate
8 ounces vodka
8 ounces cherry schnapps

Make lemonade in pitcher. Stir in liquor. Refrigerate. Serve over ice in chilled cocktail glasses.

Pop the Cherry

4 ounces orange juice
2 ounces cherry brandy

Mix ingredients in cocktail shaker. Serve over ice in chilled cocktail glasses. Garnish with cherry.

Sea Breeze

46-ounce can grapefruit juice
8 ounces vodka
8 ounces cranberry juice

Mix ingredients in pitcher. Refrigerate. Serve over ice in chilled cocktail glasses.

Shoot 'Em Cowgirl

The following shot recipes are known to alter egos. Proceed with caution.

Between the Sheets

1 ounce brandy
1 ounce triple sec
1 ounce light rum

Mix ingredients over cracked ice in cocktail shaker. Strain and serve.

Blow Job

1½ ounces Kahlua
1½ ounces Irish cream liqueur
whipped topping

Fill shot glass with Kahlua and Irish cream liqueur. Add whipped topping. The *way* you drink this shot is part of its charm. Pick up the shot glass with your mouth, tip your head back, and swallow.

French Kiss

1 ounce white creme de cacao
1 ounce amaretto
1 ounce Irish cream liqueur

Mix ingredients over cracked ice in cocktail shaker. Strain and serve.

Hop, Skip, and Go Naked

1 ounce almond liqueur
1 ounce melon liqueur
1 ounce amaretto
1 ounce Irish cream liqueur

Mix ingredients over cracked ice in cocktail shaker. Strain and serve.

Horny Toad

1 ounce Irish cream liqueur
1 ounce triple sec
1 ounce Kahlua

Mix ingredients over cracked ice in cocktail shaker. Strain and serve.

Italian Stallion

1 ounce almond liqueur
1 ounce white creme de cacao
1 ounce Irish cream liqueur

Mix ingredients over cracked ice in cocktail shaker. Strain and serve.

Jell-O Shots

3-ounce package gelatin mix (any flavor)
vodka
water

Follow directions on box of gelatin mix, substituting vodka for *cold* water. Pour mixture into disposable cups. Chill in refrigerator to set.
Yield: 8 2-ounce shots

Variation: For unique gelatin molds, see the Novelty Chocolates section on page 107.

Lick it, Slam it, Suck it
tequila
salt
lime
good-looking guy's neck

Find a cute guy. Wet his neck and apply salt. Put a lime wedge between his lips, pulp facing out. Lick salt from his neck, slam tequila shot, and suck juice from his lime wedge.

One Bad Apple
apples
lemon juice
3 ounces apple juice
2 ounces apple brandy
½ ounce amaretto
1 tablespoon applesauce

Core apples to form small shot glasses. Coat inside of apples with lemon juice to prevent browning and refrigerate. Mix other ingredients in blender with ice and pour into apple shot glasses. Garnish with cinnamon sticks.

Panty Remover
1½ ounces sloe gin
1½ ounces Kahlua

Mix ingredients over cracked ice in cocktail shaker. Strain and serve.

Screaming Orgasm
1½ ounces Irish cream liqueur
1 ounce vodka
½ ounce Kahlua
whipped topping

Mix first three ingredients over cracked ice in cocktail shaker. Strain and serve with whipped topping.

Safe Sex on the Beach
1 ounce peach nectar
1 ounce cranberry juice
1 ounce orange juice

Mix ingredients over cracked ice in cocktail shaker. Strain and serve.

Sex on the Beach

2 ounces cranberry juice
¾ ounce peach schnapps
¾ ounce vodka
½ ounce orange juice

Mix ingredients over cracked ice in cocktail shaker. Strain and serve.

Slime

1 cup water
3-ounce package lime gelatin
½ cup melon liqueur
½ cup vodka

Boil water and add to gelatin in bowl. Stir in melon liqueur and vodka.
Pour gelatin mixture into disposable cups. Chill in refrigerator to set.
Yield: 8 2-ounce shots

Slippery Nipple

1½ ounces butterscotch schnapps
1½ ounces Irish cream liqueur
dash grenadine

Top schnapps with Irish cream liqueur in chilled shot glass. Add dash of
grenadine to center.

Spit or Swallow

1½ ounces coconut rum
1½ ounces banana liqueur
½ ounce milk

Mix first two ingredients over cracked ice in cocktail shaker. Top with milk, strain ice, and serve.

When Life Hands You Lemons, Make Shots

1½ ounces Absolut Citron
1½ ounces sweet and sour
1 slice lemon
½ teaspoon sugar

Mix first two ingredients over cracked ice in cocktail shaker. Strain and serve. Drink shot, then suck lemon sprinkled with sugar. For a unique shot glass, hollow out a lemon and coat the rim with sugar.

Wild Banana Banshee

1 ounce banana liqueur
1 ounce white creme de cacao
1 ounce cream

Mix ingredients over cracked ice in cocktail shaker. Strain and serve.

Drink Garnishes

Provide guests with a variety of funny stickers so they can personalize their glasses, making them easier to find throughout the evening. Also, enhance the exotic drink recipes with the following accessories.

Condom *Cocktail* Drink Stirrers

Insert a plastic cocktail stirrer or fruit-flavored candy stick into the center of a nonlubricated condom. Tie off with colorful curling ribbon.

Here's Your Cherry

Attach personalized labels to long-stemmed cherries. For example, write, "Jan's Cherry" on the label.

Fancy Ice Cubes

Cut strawberries in half to resemble hearts and freeze in slots of ice cube trays. For best results, fill ice trays one-fourth full with distilled water, add garnishes, and freeze. Remove tray, fill to the top with water, and freeze again. For a flavorful and decorative touch, freeze fruit juices in ice trays.

Novelty-Shaped Ice Molds

Purchase X-rated ice cube trays at your local adult novelty store.

Crazy Straws

Supplies:
- Craft foam sheets
- Scissors
- Straws

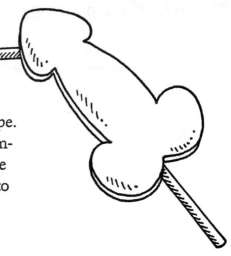

Directions: Cut foam into desired shape. See page 119 of the Appendix for template. Cut small slit in center of shape for straw insertion, or mount shape to straw with double-sided sticky pad.

Confetti

Cut an orange into quarters and remove fruit. Slice peels into thin strips and skewer strips on toothpicks with pieces of star fruit.

Toasts

To the men (bride's name)'s loved,
To the men (bride's name)'s kissed;
And her heartfelt apologies
To the men she's missed.
—*Anonymous*

A toast to love and laughter and happily ever after.
—*Old Wedding Toast*

Here's to the land we love and the love we land.
—*Anonymous*

Never go to bed mad;
Stay up and fight.
—*Phyllis Diller*

Women have many faults,
Men have only two;
Just everything they say,
And everything they do.
—*Anonymous*

Marriage is a wonderful institution,
But who wants to live in an institution?
—*Groucho Marx*

Beauty lies in the hands of the beerholder.
—*Anonymous*

Time is never wasted when you're wasted all the time.
—*Anonymous*

When we drink, we get drunk.
When we're drunk, we fall asleep.
When we're asleep, we commit no sin.
When we commit no sin, we go to heaven.
So, let's all get drunk and go to heaven!
—*Old Irish Toast*

Here's to being single,
Drinking doubles,
And seeing triple.
—*Anonymous*

May your wedding night be like a kitchen table:
Four legs and no drawers.
—*Old Irish Toast*

On the chest of a barmaid in Sale
Were tattooed the prices of ale.
And on her behind,
For the sake of the blind,
Was the same information in braille.
—*Anonymous*

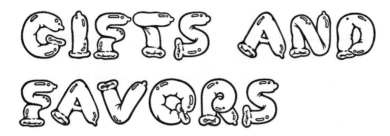

GIFTS AND FAVORS

Here are fun gift ideas for the guest of honor and party favors for the bachelorettes.

Theme Gifts for the Bride

A gift-giving theme will allow your guests to be creative. Here are several directions you can take.

All White

To salute the fair maiden who's about to be wed, have everyone give her something white as a tribute to her virginity. (We know what you're thinking, but don't worry. As long as your friend is not marrying the King of England, no one will ever know the difference.)

Pack Her Bags

Scour flea markets for an old suitcase. Post a sign that reads, "Hawaii or Bust" on the outside of the suitcase. Ask guests to bring items that the bride should take on her honeymoon. Put these items in the suitcase and have the bride unpack them at the party. Select items relevant to the honeymoon destination. For example, a Latin-American Spanish phrase book would be useful for the bride who's headed to Mexico.

Contemporary Wishing Well

Transform the tradition of the bridal-shower wishing well, a custom that called for each guest to contribute a basic household item, such as toilet paper or a bar of soap, to the newlywed's "wishing well." For a contemporary twist, purchase a special container for the bride and invite guests to fill it with inexpensive gifts. For example, buy a travel bag for the honeymoon and have each guest contribute a travel-size toiletry. Or, fill a grocery bag with nonperishable aphrodisiacs.

Memory Basket

Send blank index cards with invitations asking each guest to jot down anonymously a memory she's shared with the bride. Ask her to tie the card to some memento from that occasion. For example, a bottle of Palmolive should remind the bride of the night her friend put dish-washing soap in the hot tub at her apartment complex. A roll of toilet paper might recall memories of the night the bride and her friend decorated a favorite math teacher's front yard. Make it extra fun by challenging the bride to guess which guest brought each memory.

Finish the Phrase

Assign each guest the task of completing a phrase such as "A romantic day at...." She must also provide gifts for the bride that correspond to the phrase. For example, if a guest's completed phrase is "A romantic day at the park," she might give the bride an inexpensive tablecloth, a bottle of wine, and two plastic toasting glasses. If she chooses "A romantic day at the beach," then his-and-her beach towels would be fitting gifts. Encourage creative interpretations and award prizes.

Every Day's a Holiday

Assign each guest a holiday and ask her to bring presents to help the bride romantically celebrate that holiday. For example, the guest who gets the Fourth of July may choose to contribute red, white, and blue thong underwear. As a present topper, she may attach a small package of fireworks with a note that reads, "Happy Fourth of July! Here's everything you need to enjoy the fireworks!"

Stock the Liquor Cabinet

Invite each guest to bring her favorite drink recipe and some utensil or bottle of alcohol required to make it. Consider a blender or set of wineglasses as a group gift. Don't forget to try out the recipes!

It's All in a Word

Pick a word related to love, sex, or marriage that has the same number of letters as the number of expected guests. Assign a letter from that word to each guest and ask her to bring sexy presents that begin with that letter.

For example, if you're expecting seven guests at the party, consider the word *massage*. The guest assigned the letter M could give the bride some set of *matching* items, *music* CDs, *massage* lotion, and so on.

Easy-to-Make Gifts for the Bride

Handcrafted gifts are always treasured. Here are a few suggestions.

Time Capsule

Paint an extra-large popcorn tin in the bride's colors. Stencil the couple's names on the outside along with the current year. Place a variety of items in the tin including a newspaper from the day of the bachelorette party, a menu from the restaurant where you dined, a shot glass from your favorite bar, a popular CD, fad memorabilia, letters from each guest to the bride, and so on. You might want to have guests fill out a questionnaire about the couple's future and place them in the tin. You could also videotape the party and drop the tape in the tin when the night draws to a close. Seal the tin and tell the bride she can open it on a designated wedding anniversary.

Pillow Talk

Make a unique pillow, preferably in the colors of the newlywed's bedroom. Embroider or use fabric paint to write "Tonight" on one side of the pillow and "Not tonight" on the other.

Honeymoon Scrapbook

Buy a scrapbook for the bride and decoupage a picture of the honeymoon destination on the front cover. Give each guest a page from the scrapbook to decorate and personalize. Supply necessary craft scissors, colored construction paper, glue, glitter, and markers if you'll be performing this activity at the party. Award prizes for the most creative pages.

Coupon Book

Have guests make unique love coupons for the bride. Place them in a special coupon file. The bride can present these coupons to her groom for redemption whenever she likes. Be creative.

Variation: Have guests write romantic suggestions on slips of paper and place them in a jar. The bride and groom can select one periodically to enjoy some unexpected romance. Favorite slips can be recycled.

Easy-to-Make Favors for Guests

Craft your own party favors to make a unique impression.

Virginal Body Oils and Splashes

Buy small empty decorative bottles from your local craft store and fill them with homemade body-soothing concoctions. To make a refreshing splash, mix 6 ounces of water with 1 tablespoon of rubbing alcohol and 1 teaspoon of a lavender-scented essential oil. You'll find essential oils wherever herbal remedies are sold. To make a soothing oil, add ½ teaspoon of an essential oil, such as geranium, to 2 ounces of a base oil such as jojoba. Geranium is a natural tonic believed to prevent mood swings and PMS. Decorate the bottles with homemade labels containing the name of the magic potion and exaggerated claims such as, "Guaranteed to bring back your virginity."

Variation: Buy bottles of lotion or bath splash and replace the label with a personalized version named after the bride.

Party Pics

Using foam core, design a humorous photo frame with cut-out heads. Have an artist paint cartoon versions of scantly clad, well-endowed, beautiful women toasting. One might be wearing a veil. Guests can place their heads through the cutouts and pose for the camera. Send pictures home as party favors.

Rubber Jewelry

Supplies:
- Clear vinyl
- Scissors
- Embellishments such as beads, buttons, ribbon, and glitter
- Condoms
- Clear-drying craft glue or clear nonfrost tape
- Fabric paint
- Jewelry-making supplies such as pin backs and earring hooks

back

Directions: Form basic jewelry designs by cutting clear vinyl into pairs of desired shapes. Sandwich embellishments and condoms between the pairs of vinyl pieces. Secure vinyl edges with glue or tape. Decorate with fabric paint or other embellishments. Create pieces of jewelry from the finished pieces by attaching pin backs or earring hooks. Vinyl and jewelry-making accessories are available in craft and fabric stores.

X-rated Fortune Cookies

Create customized fortune cookies using the following recipe and fill with fantasy fortunes.

6 tablespoons butter
6 tablespoons sugar
2 egg whites
1 teaspoon almond extract
⅔ cup flour
20 fortunes written on tiny slips of paper (about ½ by 2½ inches)

Preheat oven to 400°F. Blend butter, sugar, egg whites, and almond extract in a mixer. Fold in flour. Evenly space four balls of batter (each measuring approximately 1½ teaspoons) onto greased cookie sheet. Use back of spoon to spread balls into thin 3-inch circles. Bake for 4 minutes or until edges start to become golden. Use spatula to remove one cookie at a time to work space. Place fortune in middle of cookie. To make traditional fortune-cookie shape, gather opposite edges of cookie together and hold for a few seconds. Next, push nonpressed side edges of cookie downward while using thumbs to press center upward. You will need to work fast as cookies will harden quickly. Repeat baking process with rest of dough on cooled cookie sheets.

Boyfriend in a Bag

Cut out pictures from *Playgirl* and paste to plain paper bags. Give each cutout a name such as "Bob the Banker." Include his vital statistics in the bag along with cards signed from him to the bachelorette and phone messages such as, "Just called to say I love you." This is the perfect gift for single bachelorettes who are too frequently asked, "Do you have a boyfriend?"

PMS Survival Kits

Gather the following items: a chocolate candy bar, jelly beans in a medicine bottle labeled "PMS Antidote—For minor relief of major bitchiness," and a shot glass. Include a roll of yellow tape such as that found at crime scenes, or make your own from yellow crepe paper with "Warning...PMS...Do Not Cross" written on it. Wrap the items in cellophane and attach a note card that humorously describes the contents.

Chocolate Kiss Rosebuds

Supplies for each rosebud:
- 2 chocolate kisses
- 5-inch-square piece of red cellophane
- 18-inch piece of sturdy floral wire
- Green floral tape
- Silk rose leaf

Directions: To form rosebud, place 2 chocolate kisses (bottoms together) in center of square piece of cellophane. Draw up 4 corners around the kisses, twist corners, and secure. Attach wrapped kisses to floral wire with floral tape. Cover entire piece of wire to form flower stem. Attach silk rose leaf to stem with floral tape. Rosebuds can be placed in vase with baby's breath and fresh greens to form centerpiece.

Panty Rose

Supplies for each rose:
- Pair of skimpy underwear
- Straight pins
- 18-inch piece of sturdy floral wire
- Green floral tape
- Silk rose leaf

Directions: Roll underwear into tight bud and secure with straight pins. Cover one end of floral wire with green floral tape to prevent it from snagging panty. Insert covered end into rolled panty. Secure panty rose to floral wire by wrapping with floral tape. (See previous Chocolate Kiss Rosebud illustration.) Cover entire piece of wire with floral tape to form flower stem. Attach silk rose leaf to stem with floral tape.

Romance in a Can

Save old coffee cans. Clean and decorate with acrylic paint. Line cans with colorful tissue paper and fill with items such as votive candles, romantic CDs and books, and samples of body lotions and bubble bath.

Men's Boxer Shorts Tote Bags

Supplies for each bag:
- Pair of boxer shorts
- 2 strips of coordinating fabric for tote handles
- Thread in coordinating color
- Fabric paint

Directions: Sew the legs and fly of the boxer shorts closed. Attach shoulder straps to waistband. Using fabric paint, personalize the bag with party details.

Other *Favorite* Ideas for Guests

Here are more keepsakes to help you treasure this party of a lifetime.

Shot Glasses

Give each bachelorette a shot glass. Attach the recipe for a Blow Job or Screaming Orgasm. Check out shot recipes starting on page 87.

Pretty Prophylactic Surprises

Give each bachelorette a condom wrapped in gold foil. Tie off the package with fancy ribbon featuring the bride's name and the party date. You're certain to catch guests by surprise as they unwrap the seemingly elegant party favor.

Personalized Gifts

Order customized T-shirts or sweatshirts to commemorate your special occasion, or make them yourself with fabric paint or embroidery. Also, consider having drink huggies printed for your party.

Novelty Chocolates

Place an order for erotic chocolates from Chocolate Fantasies online at http://chocolatefantasies.com or call toll-free at 800-595-9936. If you'd like to make uniquely shaped chocolates, call Discovery II, Inc., Cake and Candy Supplies toll-free at 877-358-8068. This company offers naughty and nice candy molds that can be used to make chocolates, gelatins, or ice cubes.

MORE PARTY IDEAS

Weddings have inspired lots of fun celebrations throughout the centuries. Here's a look at something old—the bachelor party—and something new—the party combo.

The Bachelor Party

The bachelor party tradition hasn't changed much in several hundred years. The Spartans were among the first to initiate the idea of the groom gathering with his best friends before the wedding for a special farewell supper, originally called the men's mess.

Today's groom might find himself in a different sort of mess if the farewell celebration is scheduled too close to the wedding. For all the reasons previously mentioned, scheduling parties too close to the wedding may pose all kinds of problems. Consequently, this male bonding ritual now occurs several days—if not weeks—in advance. After all, even the most resilient and resourceful bachelor needs time to sober up, find his ride home, and recover.

Normally, the best planning advice for a bachelor party is, "Keep it simple." The best man usually hosts the event and invitations are generally extended over the phone. If written invitations are sent, they typically involve a wadded-up piece of paper inviting bachelors to get trashed.

One of the few gallant traditions of the bachelor party calls for the groom to propose a toast to his bride at some point during the evening. Guests often break their glasses after the toast to insure they will never be used for a less meaningful purpose. While booze and strippers do seem to be the stereotypical staples of the bachelor party, here are some fresh alternatives.

Fishing Tournament

In honor of your buddy's big catch, go deep-sea fishing or cast your lines closer to home at an area lake or pond. Send invitations attached to lures. Give the guys personalized fishing caps. You could also celebrate in the great outdoors with a white-water rafting adventure or hunting expedition.

Let's Get Sauced

Invite the guys to a barbecue. Have lots of chilled beer on hand and grill brats or make-your-own kebabs. Send each bachelor home with a jar of your secret barbecue sauce.

Take A Shot

Stuff party details in shot glasses inviting bachelors to enjoy a tequila-tasting party. Host the festivities at a Mexican restaurant or on the sandy beaches of Cancun. Wherever you end up, make the groom wear a sombrero.

Get Lucky

Send party details attached to casino chips or on card stock cut in the shape of dice inviting bachelors to get lucky. They'll need luck for an evening of craps, blackjack, roulette, and so on.

Take Him Out to the Ball Game

The groom's days of playing the field are numbered, so what better place to say farewell than the ball park? Write party details on base-balls. Arrange for the special occasion to be recognized on the scoreboard and also by an appearance of the team mascot.

You're Screwed

Tape screws to the invitations. Shower the groom with tools and other hardware items, and toast his pending marriage with screwdrivers.

The Party Combo

Consider combining the two parties for some major coed fun. Here are a few sample party-combo themes.

Retro Party

For invitations to this throwback party, write details on record labels placed on old 45s. Mail in padded envelopes. Dress the bride and groom in bridal attire from the years they were born and invite bridal party members and other guests to sport the same garb. Visit flea markets and vintage clothing shops to find the perfect party apparel. You could also invite guests to dress like celebrities popular from that time. Award prizes, such as eight-track tapes and old posters, to the best-dressed retro guests. Stay in theme throughout the party with period music, food, decorations, games, and so on.

Tea & Tee Party

Combine the traditions of tea parties and golf. For invitations, attach party details to a tea bag and bag of tees. Send each guest home with a teacup and note card explaining the cup's significance to marriage. In the early 1900s, a gentleman would often give his fiancée a teacup when the two became engaged with the promise that if ever the two were apart, she would drink from the cup and think of him. Order personalized golf towels for the guests or give each a sleeve of balls. Arrange to gather for tea after guests have completed their rounds of golf.

Costume Party

Invite guests to come dressed as their favorite celebrity couples. For invitations, find pictures of famous couples and cover their heads with photo cutouts of the bride and groom's heads. Include cartoonlike conversation bubbles into which party details have been written. At the party, include Hollywood touches such as rolling out red carpet and presenting awards for the best costumes. Have guests bring gifts that correspond to their celebrity couple such as certificates to The Sharper Image if they came dressed as James Bond and one of his women. Play Famous Couples Charades (page 115) and commemorate this celebrity bash with lots of party pics.

Greek Party

Host a toga party to pay tribute to the bride and groom's Greek matchmaker, Eros, better known by his Roman name, Cupid. Incorporate the Greek alphabet into invitations and party favors. Recruit the help of fraternity or sorority members if you get stuck. For example, make up a fraternity name such as *Kappa Iota Sigma Sigma* in which the first letters spell the word *kiss*. For personalized fun, pretend your fictitious fraternity is located at (groom's last name) University. Crown the bride with an ivy wreath and attach a tulle veil. Serve gyros and other mouthwatering Greek cuisine. Have T-shirts and plastic cups printed for take-home favors.

Variation: Throw a toga beach party in honor of Aphrodite, the goddess believed to have been born from the sea. Many seafoods are considered aphrodisiacs, so prepare a seafood bar and see what happens.

Wild West Party

Send party details attached to toy guns. Invite guests to wear western attire and attach a tulle veil to the bride's cowboy hat. Brand guests with name tags, establishing one brand for the bride's guests and another for the groom's. Barbecue steaks from a makeshift chuck wagon and serve horseshoe cake for good luck. Dance the night away at the bride and groom's favorite country-western bar. Hire an instructor to teach guests a new country dance step. Challenge guests to a bull riding or roping contest, or stage a down-the-hatch shooting match with our shot recipes (page 87). Turn tot-sized cowboy hats into goodie bags and fill with shot glasses and personalized bandannas to commemorate this special occasion.

Get a Clue Party

Separate into bachelor and bachelorette groups, then send one party on a hunt to find the other. While one group remains stationary, the other follows a trail of clues. For example, if the guys are looking for the girls, a pair of panty hose tied to one of the guy's cars could hold the first clue. From there, a trail of female-related items will eventually lead the guys to the bachelorette party already in progress.

Coed Games

While many of the games described in Chapter 3 can be played in mixed company, here are several games specifically designed for both sexes.

Famous Couples Charades

In this game of charades, the only topic is "famous couples." Contestants perform charades in coed pairs and get help from a prop box prepared by the party hostess before the party. The box contains simple disguises along with construction paper and scissors so guests can quickly design their props. Each pair will have three minutes to prepare for acting out the famous couple they've been assigned. Examples could include Jane and Tarzan, Jack and Jill, Adam and Eve, Bonnie and Clyde, Fred and Wilma, and so on. Award a prize to the guest who solves the most charades, or split the crowd into teams and award a prize to the team with the lowest overall time.

Cop a Feel

Seat five men including the groom in chairs facing the group. Blindfold the bride and challenge her to find her honey by feeling the men's chests. Once she's determined which one she thinks is her groom, spin her around and have her cop another feel of each man to make sure. After she's decided, spin her around one last time and have the groom quietly stand on his chair. When she's asked to cop one last feel of him, she'll certainly hope she's got the right one as she finds herself feeling below the belt rather than above!

The String Game

Divide guests into two teams. Give each team a piece of string (making sure the pieces are the same length). The object of the game is for team members to thread the string up and down through their clothing until all members are connected. The team with the longest piece of leftover string wins. The closer the team members stand together, the less string they'll consume. You might want to attach a spoon or other item to the end of the string to ease the threading process. Award prizes to members of the winning team.

This Is How You *Do It*

Divide guests into teams and designate captains. Have captains stand at the opposite end of the room from their teams. Place a broomstick between each captain's legs with the handle pointing toward team members. Give all team members a roll of toilet paper. Team members must walk one at a time to their captain with the roll of toilet paper between their legs and place the roll on the broom handle without using their hands. The first team to place all their rolls on their captain's broom handle wins.

Appendix

Traditional Anniversary Gifts

First: Paper

Second: Cotton

Third: Leather

Fourth: Silk, Fruit, or Flowers

Fifth: Wood

Sixth: Iron or Candy

Seventh: Copper or Wool

Eighth: Bronze

Ninth: Pottery

Tenth: Tin or Aluminum

Eleventh: Steel

Twelfth: Linen or Silk

Thirteenth: Lace

Fourteenth: Ivory

Fifteenth: Crystal

Twentieth: China

Twenty-fifth: Silver

Thirtieth: Pearl

Thirty-fifth: Coral or Jade

Fortieth: Ruby

Forty-fifth: Sapphire

Fiftieth: Gold

Fifty-fifth: Emerald

Sixtieth & Seventy-fifth: Diamonds

The Guest List

Name

Mailing Address

Phone Number/E-mail Address

Name

Mailing Address

Phone Number/E-mail Address

Name

Mailing Address

Phone Number/E-mail Address

Name

Mailing Address

Phone Number/E-mail Address

Name

Mailing Address

Phone Number/E-mail Address

Name

Mailing Address

Phone Number/E-mail Address

Anatomically Correct Template

This template can be used in a variety of ways. Make uniquely shaped sugar cookies using the recipe found on page 78. Or, make luminarias by tracing the design onto paper bags. Cut the design from the bags with a sharp knife or scissors. Fill each bag with sand and a votive candle.

$\mathcal{B}$	$\mathcal{L}$	$\mathcal{M}$	$\mathcal{B}$	$\mathcal{O}$
		FREE		

Hungman

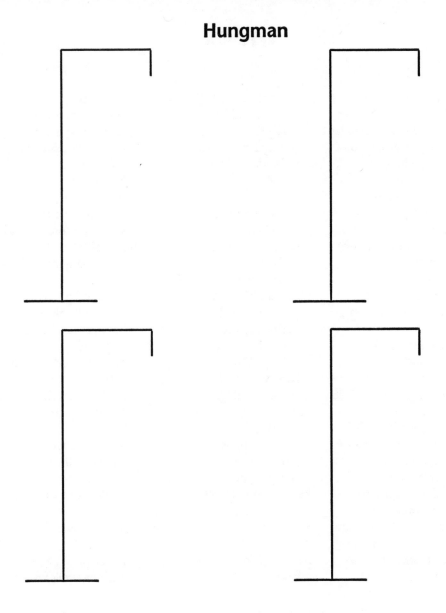

Index

The Best Bachelorette Party Games & Activities

by Courtney Cooke

Here's a great way to liven up any bachelorette party: five group activities and four pencil games that are a bit risqué but absolutely hilarious. Each game comes with duplicate game sheets for eight guests.

Order #6073

The Best Bridal Shower Party Games #1

by Courtney Cooke

Here's all you need to get your bridal shower off to a fast and funny start: four pencil games that everyone will enjoy (with duplicate game sheets for eight people) plus four entertaining group activities.

Order #6060

The Best Bridal Shower Party Games #2

by Courtney Cooke

Here's a second book of party games guaranteed to make your shower a hit: four pencil games that everyone will enjoy (with duplicate game sheets for eight people) plus four entertaining group activities.

Order #6068

The Best Baby Shower Book
by Courtney Cooke

This contemporary guide for planning baby showers is packed with helpful hints, delicious recipes, checklists, designs for invitations and name tags, decorating ideas, a "wish list" for the mother-to-be, and party games that are fun without being juvenile.

Order #1239

The Best Wedding Shower Book
by Courtney Cooke

This guide helps make wedding showers fun. It includes dozens of delicious recipes and menu ideas, imaginative shower themes, suggestions for gifts and decorations that don't cost a bundle, creative concepts for couples' showers, practical party-planning checklists, and fun party games that won't embarrass your guests.

Order #6059

The Complete Wedding Planner
by Edith Gilbert

In this comprehensive guide, you'll find authoritative information on every aspect of a wedding, from the engagement to the honeymoon. This book offers practical, up-to-date guidance on selecting rings; planning a rehearsal; wording invitations and announcements; managing a budget; selecting wedding attire; organizing a reception; choosing attendants; coping with florists, musicians, and photographers; and much more.

Order #6005

Storybook Weddings
by Robin A. Kring

Here are 50 wedding themes that will help the bride and groom create a spectacular event. You'll find creative, theme-appropriate ideas for invitations; fashions and costumes for the bride, groom, and wedding party; elegant décor suggestions for the ceremony and reception; and imaginative entertainment and menu concepts. Each theme is packed with ideas designed to create memories that will be cherished well beyond the couple's golden anniversary.

Order #6010

Look for Meadowbrook Press books where you buy books.
You may also order books by using the form printed below.

Order Form

Qty.	Title	Author	Order #	Unit Cost (U.S. $)	Total
	Best Party Book	Warner, P.	6089	$9.00	
	Best Baby Shower Book	Cooke, C.	1239	$7.00	
	Best Baby Shower Party Games #1	Cooke, C.	6063	$3.95	
	Best Bachelorette Party Games & Activities	Cooke, C.	6073	$3.95	
	Best Bridal Shower Party Games #1	Cooke, C.	6060	$3.95	
	Best Bridal Shower Party Games #2	Cooke, C.	6068	$3.95	
	Best Wedding Shower Book	Cooke, C.	6059	$7.00	
	Complete Wedding Planner	Gilbert, E.	6005	$15.00	
	Dinner Party Cookbook	Brown, K.	6035	$9.00	
	For Better And For Worse	Lansky, B.	4000	$7.00	
	Games People Play	Warner, P.	6093	$8.00	
	Joy of Marriage	Dodds, M. & B.	3504	$7.00	
	Lovesick	Lansky, B.	4045	$7.00	
	Pick A Party	Sachs, P.	6085	$9.00	
	Pick-A-Party Cookbook	Sachs, P.	6086	$11.00	
	Something Old, Something New	Long, B.	6011	$9.95	
	Storybook Weddings	Kring, R.	6010	$8.00	
				Subtotal	
			Shipping and Handling (see below)		
			MN residents add 6.5% sales tax		
				Total	

YES! Please send me the books indicated above. Add $2.00 shipping and handling for the first book with a retail price up to $9.99 or $3.00 for the first book with a retail price over $9.99. Add $1.00 shipping and handling for each additional book. All orders must be prepaid. Most orders are shipped within two days by U.S. Mail (7–9 delivery days). Rush shipping is available for an extra charge. Overseas postage will be billed. **Quantity discounts available upon request.**

Send book(s) to:

Name _____ Address_____

City _____ State ___ Zip _____ Telephone (____)_____

Payment via:

❑ Check or money order payable to Meadowbrook Press

❑ Visa (for orders over $10.00 only) ❑ MasterCard (for orders over $10.00 only)

Account # _____ Signature _____ Exp. Date _____

You can also phone or fax us with a credit card order.

A FREE Meadowbrook Press catalog is available upon request.

Mail to: Meadowbrook Press, 5451 Smetana Drive, Minnetonka, MN 55343

Phone 612-930-1100   Toll-Free 800-338-2232   Fax 612-930-1940

For more information (and fun) visit our website: www.meadowbrookpress.com